17th Century Dutch Painting

17th Century Dutch Painting

Raising the Curtain on New England Private Collections

James A. Welu

Worcester Art Museum
Worcester, Massachusetts

Library of Congress Card Catalogue Number: 79-64580
Copyright 1979 Worcester Art Museum and James A. Welu.
All rights reserved
Published in 1979
Printed in the United States of America
Worcester Art Museum, Worcester, Massachusetts 01608

cover: Johannes Hannot *Still Life with Lobster*

Foreword

In assembling the exhibition *17th Century Dutch Painting: Raising the Curtain on New England Private Collections*, the Worcester Art Museum seeks to bring to the attention of both a general audience and students of Dutch painting a number of notable works in private hands in this region. Since relatively few of the paintings are published or have been exhibited, considerable exploration was necessary to locate works for the exhibition. Several of the works were brought to the Museum's attention over the years by their owners; most, however, were located by contacting art dealers and scholars in the field.

An equally imposing problem was the inherent fragility of the paintings, particularly those on wooden panels. In order to mitigate possible dangers from climatic extremes, the exhibition was scheduled for early fall. A further concern in a day when thefts of art have become all too common was security; to this end all lenders agreed to anonymity.

Generous support to meet the costs of the exhibition has been provided by the Thom McAn Company of Worcester, Mr. and Mrs. Emil Eisenberg, and the National Endowment for the Arts. The Museum gratefully acknowledges this assistance as well as the kind cooperation of the individual lenders to the exhibition.

Dr. James A. Welu, organizer and cataloguer of *17th Century Dutch Painting*, has spent almost two years preparing the exhibition. His efforts to present unknown and rarely seen paintings of high quality from an era that produced more distinguished painters than perhaps any other have resulted in an exceptional exhibition—one that not only represents a significant contribution to art historical scholarship, but that also gives the public an opportunity to view a wide range of fine works from "The Golden Age of Dutch Painting."

Richard Stuart Teitz
Director, Worcester Art Museum

Acknowledgments

I would like to extend my warm gratitude to the lenders who have made this exhibition possible. I appreciate their generosity in making their paintings available for not only the exhibition, but also the preliminary examinations and photography necessary for the catalogue.

Numerous individuals are to be thanked for information used in writing the catalogue. Many of these persons are mentioned in the various entries. I owe very special thanks to Timothy A. Riggs for reading over the manuscript and providing numerous insightful comments. Many of my colleagues in Dutch art also offered helpful suggestions; I would like to acknowledge, in particular, Albert Blankert and Otto Naumann. The research for the catalogue would never have been possible without the valuable material made available to me at the Frick Art Reference Library in New York, the Rijksbureau voor Kunsthistorische Documentatie in The Hague, and the Witt Library of the Courtauld Institute in London. I appreciate the kind assistance received from the staffs of these and many other institutions both here and abroad.

Worcester Art Museum Conservators Helen Mar Parkin and Norman E. Muller are to be thanked for examining most of the paintings and for undertaking conservation work on several of them. For many of the photographs, I am also grateful to both conservators and to Herbert B. Walden. A special debt of gratitude is owed to Gaye L. Brown for her excellent editing and many fine suggestions.

For their sponsorship of various aspects of the exhibition, I am grateful to Thom McAn Company of Worcester, Mr. and Mrs. Emil Eisenberg, and the National Endowment for the Arts. Finally, I would like to express my deep appreciation to the staff of the Worcester Art Museum whose cooperative spirit has been an important factor in the realization of this exhibition.

J. A. Welu

List of Abbreviations

HdG	Hofstede de Groot, C. *A Catalogue Raisonné of the Works of the Most Eminent Dutch Painters of the Seventeenth Century Based on the Work of John Smith.* Translated and edited by E. G. Hawke. Vols. 1–8. London: Macmillan, 1907–27. Idem. *Beschreibendes und kritisches Verzeichnis der Werke der hervorragendsten holländischen Maler des XVII. Jahrhunderts.* Vols. 9,10. Esslingen a N.: Paul Neff Verlag, 1926–28.
Houbraken	Houbraken, A. *De groote schouburgh der Nederlantsche konstschilders en schilderessen.* 3 vols. Amsterdam: A. Houbraken, 1718–21.
RKD	Rijksbureau voor Kunsthistorische Documentatie, The Hague
Tot lering en vermaak	Jongh, E. de; Bedaux, Jan Baptist; Hecht, Peter; Stumpel, Jeroen; and Vos, Rik. *Tot lering en vermaak.* Exhibition catalogue. Amsterdam: Rijksmuseum, 1976.
Witt	Witt Library, Courtauld Institute, University of London, London

Introduction

When the Worcester Art Museum undertook the idea of organizing a show of seventeenth-century Dutch painting, we hoped to document some of the more important, but little-known works in private collections throughout the New England area. The forty paintings that were eventually chosen for the exhibition represent approximately one-third of the total number examined. Drawn from eighteen different collections, these works were selected not only for their quality, but also to show as many aspects as possible of seventeenth-century Dutch painting. All of the major centers of Dutch painting are represented: Amsterdam, Haarlem, Utrecht, Leiden, Delft, and The Hague. The range of subjects is equally comprehensive and includes marines, landscapes, portraits, still lifes, genre and architectural scenes, and biblical and mythological themes. Some categories of subject matter are represented by four or five works spread throughout the century which help to give an idea of the overall development within the individual genre.

As to be expected in a show of this kind, several of the major artists are missing, but in most cases their influence can be seen in works by the so-called minor masters. The influence of Rembrandt is particularly evident in two paintings from the late 1640s, one by Egbert van der Poel, the other by Rombout van Troyen. Likewise, the circle of Jacob van Ruisdael is represented by Claes Molenaer and Jan Wijnants.

Because most of the paintings in the exhibition have rarely, if ever, been exhibited or published in the past, a special effort has been made to provide full documentation on each of them. In the course of the research for the show, several of the works were reattributed, and in many instances additional provenance was uncovered. Since many of the painters represented in the exhibition will be unfamiliar to the general public, we have provided summary biographies, some of which include new information on the artist. In preparation for the exhibition, several paintings underwent conservation treatment, and many were furnished with more appropriate frames.

The title of the show was suggested by the seventeenth-century Dutch practice of hanging curtains in front of paintings,[1] beautifully illustrated in Gabriel Metsu's *The Letter Reader* (fig. 1). In this typical seventeenth-century Dutch interior, a maidservant pulls back part of a curtain to look at a framed marine painting. The curtain increases the resemblance of the framed picture to a window through which a seascape can be glimpsed. Such curtains were added to paintings as a protective device, to keep off the light and dust. They also added a certain preciousness to the work, implying that it was to be exposed only when it was intended to be looked at, similar to the way in which the Chinese and Japanese view their paintings.[2] The curtains were attached by means of a cord or brass rod to the frames, which ranged from simple wooden strips to massive, carved and gilded moldings.[3]

Although not unique to the northern Netherlands, the picture-curtain enjoyed its greatest vogue there. Judging from the interior scenes in which they frequently appear, these curtains were used by the Dutch mainly

1 Gabriel Metsu, *The Letter Reader,* oil on panel, 52.5 x 40.2 cm. Blessington, Ireland, Sir Alfred Beit

2 Rembrandt, *The Holy Family (with Painted Frame and Curtain)*, 1646, oil on panel, 46.5 x 68.8 cm. Kassel, Staatliche Gemäldegalerie

around the middle of the seventeenth century. With their strong interest in illusionism, Dutch artists soon began incorporating representations of these curtains into the paintings themselves. One of the earliest examples is Rembrandt's *The Holy Family*, dated 1646 (fig. 2). This work includes a representation of not only the curtain used to cover the painting, but also the picture's ornate gold frame. By defining the foreground plane, the curtain and frame enhance the illusion of space and at the same time add to the intimacy of the scene.

The painted curtain has a long tradition in western art. According to Pliny, the Greek artist Parrhasios (ca. 400 B.C.) painted into one of his illusionistic works a curtain so convincing that his rival Zeuxis tried to remove it.[4] In Roman portraiture, a curtain pulled to the side was often used to introduce a political leader and, like a theater curtain, set him apart from the world of everyday reality. Later the same motif was used in Christian religious subjects with connotations of divine revelation. In both portraiture and religious painting, the motif persists through the Middle Ages and the Renaissance and into the seventeenth century.[5] Rembrandt may have had the Christian tradition in mind when he included the curtain in his painting of the Holy Family.

With its illusionistic possibilities, the curtain motif was a natural for *trompe l'oeil* painting, which in the Netherlands had its greatest following in Leiden. A fine example of this tradition is Johannes Hannot's *Still Life with Lobster*, featured here on the cover. The attractive green satin curtain painted into this work not only adds to the richness of the still-life objects, but also helps to create the illusion of space inside the niche.

As Reutersvärd points out,[6] in the *trompe l'oeil* use of the curtain, the emphasis on illusionism can be placed either on what lies behind the curtain, as in the still life by Hannot, or on the curtain itself. In Herman Nauwincx's *Northern Landscape with Trompe l'Oeil Curtain* (fig. 3), the feigned curtain and frame both cast shadows onto the picture plane, calling attention to its two-dimensionality. By contrast, the curtain and frame appear dramatically three-dimensional. So convincing is the illusion that, like Zeuxis, one is tempted to pull back the curtain completely in order to see the rest of the painting.

By showing part of the landscape exposed and part of it still concealed, Nauwincx suggests the curiosity and excitement associated with seeing an image formerly kept from view. In this same spirit, the Worcester Art Museum takes great delight in "raising the curtain" on the following forty paintings. Indeed, we are pleased to be able to introduce these rarely seen paintings to a wider audience and at the same time to clarify the position of each in the history of seventeenth-century Dutch art.

3 Herman Nauwincx, *Northern Landscape with Trompe l'Oeil Curtain*, oil on canvas, 78 x 91 cm. Private German collection

1 On this subject, see P. Reutersvärd, "Tavelförhänget. Kring ett motiv i holländskt 1600-talsmåleri," *Konsthistorisk Tidskrift* 25 (1956): 97–113; L. Gowing, *Vermeer* (London: Faber and Faber, 1952), pp. 99–103.

2 The curtain as a covering for an image is usually considered a western phenomenon; yet, as Valrae Reynolds points out, the curtain was a standard detail on Tibetan *tankas* of the 18th to 20th centuries (*Tibet: A Lost World*, exh. cat. [New York: The American Federation of Art, 1979], p. 93).

3 W. Martin notes one instance in which the curtain was ordered along with the frame (*Gerard Dou*, trans. Clara Bell [London: G. Bell and Sons, 1908], p. 71). The curtains appear in a variety of colors—red, blue, green, purple—and are frequently trimmed with a decorative fringe border. In some cases the curtain consisted of two pieces of cloth which were pulled to either side like a stage curtain; see Pieter Quast's interior scene last recorded in the Von Kilenyi sale, Ernst-Museum, Budapest, 26 November 1917, no. 108.

4 See E. Kris and O. Kurz, *Die Legende vom Künstler: ein geschichtlicher Versuch* (Vienna: Krystall-Verlag, 1934), p. 70.

5 For more on this subject, see the following two recently completed dissertations: J. K. Eberlein, "Apparitio regis—revelatio veritatis. Studien zur Darstellung des Vorhangs in der bildenden Kunst von der Spätantike bis zum Ende des Mittelalters" (Ph.D. diss., Universität Würzburg, 1979) and B. A. Sigel, *Der Vorhang der Sixtinischen Madonna. Herkunft und Bedeutung eines Motivs der Marienikonographie* (Ph.D. diss., Universität Zürich [Zurich: Juris Druck, 1977]).

6 Reutersvärd, "Tavelförhänget."

Ludolf Bakhuizen

Emden 1631 – 1708 Amsterdam

1

Shipping in Coastal Waters

Oil on canvas, 50 x 42.8 cm

Signed and dated lower left: LBakhuizen / 1664

Provenance: Sale, Sotheby Parke Bernet, N.Y., 7 June 1978, no. 52; private collection.

Leaving his home town in East Friesland around 1649, Bakhuizen settled in Amsterdam, where he first served as a merchant's clerk and also taught calligraphy. He soon turned to drawing, choosing as his main subject naval vessels. From drawing he turned to painting, which he studied under Allart van Everdingen and Hendrick Dubbels. Greatly influenced by Willem van de Velde the Younger, Bakhuizen became Holland's leading marine painter after Van de Velde left for England in 1672. He was patronized by the town of Amsterdam as well as numerous princes from abroad.

A relatively early work,[1] this seascape shows the influence of Van de Velde, particularly in the many picturesque outlines and simplified forms. The rowboat and barge, both filled with passengers, suggest a welcoming party for the large, incoming ship, which appears to be an Indiaman.[2] Cast into shadow, the ship forms a strong silhouette that dominates the vertical composition. Another bold design, the brightly illuminated, ochre-colored sail on the barge, provides a striking accent to the painting's overall cold, blue tonality.

From early on in his career, Bakhuizen was extremely familiar with naval vessels; yet for pictorial purposes he often took liberties in his renderings of them, as seen here in the exaggerated shape of the barge and the unusual placement of its leeboard.

---

1 It was in this year that Bakhuizen was first mentioned as a painter, having previously been referred to as a draughtsman; see C. Hofstede de Groot, *A Catalogue Raisonné of the Works of the Most Eminent Dutch Painters of the Seventeenth Century Based on the Work of John Smith*, trans. and ed. E. G. Hawke, vols. 1–8 (London: Macmillan, 1907–27),7:211 (hereafter cited as HdG).

2 For their helpful comments on the vessels in this and the other marine paintings, I am grateful to M. S. Robinson and J. van Beylen.

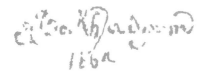

Gerrit Adriaensz. Berckheyde

Haarlem 1638 – 1698 Haarlem

2

Church of St. Cecilia, Cologne

Oil on canvas, 52.7 x 62.2 cm

Signed lower left: g Berck Heyde

Provenance: The Honorable Charles Willoughby, London; dealer, Durlacher Bros., N.Y., 1946; private collection.

Exhibitions: *A Loan Exhibition of Fifty Painters of Architecture*, Wadsworth Atheneum, Hartford, Conn., 30 October–7 December 1947, no. 3; *Works of Art Belonging to Alumnae*, Smith College Museum of Art, Northampton, Mass., June 1950, no. 5; *One Hundred: An Exhibition to Celebrate the Centennial Year of Smith College*, Smith College Museum of Art, Northampton, Mass., 1 May– 1 June 1975, no. 7.

Gerrit Berckheyde was probably a pupil of his elder brother Job Berckheyde. In their youth both brothers traveled along the Rhine in Germany, working at Cologne and Bonn and for the Elector Palatine at Heidelberg. After their return to Haarlem, Gerrit entered the Guild of St. Luke in 1660. He painted some landscapes and church interiors, but his favorite subjects were the streets, canals, and squares in his home town, Haarlem, and in Amsterdam and The Hague.

The Church of St. Cecilia in Cologne would have been seen by Berckheyde during his visit to the city in the 1650s.[1] This Romanesque structure, located in the center of old Cologne, was rebuilt in the middle of the tenth century and again in the twelfth century. Partially destroyed during World War II, the church was later restored and converted into the Schnütgen Museum.

A detail from a 1642 plan of Cologne (fig. 2a) shows that in this painting the open space and row of trees to the right of the church are the creation of the artist. In fact, except for the church, the only building that can be identified with certainty is the Rheinufer, a fish market (now destroyed), which here appears behind and immediately to the right of the church, when in fact its actual location was along the Rhine.[2]

The angle from which the church is depicted and the use of strong light and shadow all stress the medieval structure's massiveness and irregularity— attributes which are further enhanced by the row of delicate and evenly spaced trees.[3] The same church, also depicted from the northeast corner, appears in another, slightly smaller painting by Berckheyde in the Museum of Fine Arts, Boston (fig. 2b).[4] In comparison with the Boston picture, which has been dated around 1673,[5] this painting exhibits a cooler and more limited palette, stronger use of chiaroscuro, and greater simplification of planes. These factors, plus the fashionable costumes of the couple at the far left,

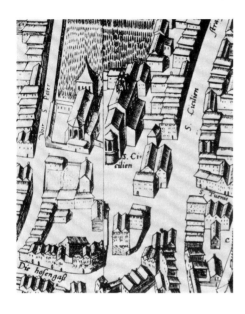

2a Detail of a plan of Cologne by Gerard Mercator, published by Henricus Hondius, Amsterdam, 1642, engraving. Historischen Museen-Kölnisches Stadtmuseum (Photo: Rheinisches Bildarchiv)

2b Gerrit Berckheyde, *The Church of St. Cecilia, Cologne*, oil on panel, 32.5 x 40.3 cm. Boston, Museum of Fine Arts, gift of Mrs. Charles Gaston Smith's Group

suggest a later date, in the 1680s or 1690s.[6] It was not unusual for Berckheyde to treat the same subject at different times throughout his career.[7]

1 Berckheyde painted many of the churches in Cologne. For a discussion and illustrations of these works, see H. Dattenberg, *Niederrheinansichten holländischen Künstler des 17.Jahrhunderts* (Düsseldorf: Rheinland-Verlag, 1967), pp. 16–43.

2 I am grateful to Dr. L. Franzheim, Kölnisches Stadtmuseum, for her comments on the buildings surrounding the church.

3 The Church of St. Cecilia seen from the same angle appears in a sketch of around 1650 by the Dutch architect Johannes Vinckboons. For an illustration, see Dattenberg, *Niederrheinansichten*, p. 340, no. 412.

4 For a discussion of the Boston painting, including topographical changes made by the artist, see C. C. Cunningham, "View of Cologne by Berckheyde," *Bulletin of the Museum of Fine Arts* 37 (1939): 3–4. A weaker version of the Boston painting is in the Dienst Verspreide Rijkscollecties, The Hague (no. NK 1702; oil on panel, 38 x 50 cm).

5 Cunningham, "Cologne," p. 3, no. 1.

6 In the 1975 Smith College exhibition, the painting was dated ca. 1670.

7 See, for example, Berckheyde's views of the market place and town hall in Haarlem, treated at least six different times between 1671 and 1691. For a summary of these works and their dates, see the entry for the Hartford painting in *Wadsworth Atheneum Paintings: The Netherlands and the German-speaking Countries, Fifteenth-Nineteenth Centuries* (Hartford: Wadsworth Atheneum, 1978), p. 119, no. 14.

Abraham van Beyeren

The Hague 1620/21 – 1690 Overschie

3

Rough Sea

Oil on cradled panel, 47.6 x 73.1 cm

Signed on leeboard of sailboat in right foreground: AVB f.

Verso: An old, illegible seal in red wax and a label inscribed *J. v. Gooyen/Gezight van't.Holl: Diep.*[1]

Provenance: Miss Emilie Grigsby, N.Y.; sale, The Anderson Auction Co., N.Y., 25 January 1912, no. 1164 (as by Jan van Goyen); John Anderson, Jr., Montclair, N.J.; sale, The American Art Association, N.Y., 6 April 1916, no. 13 (as by Jan van Goyen); bought by H. Coverdale; private collection.

Born at The Hague, Van Beyeren lived in numerous towns throughout Holland. He was in Leiden in 1639 and back in The Hague in 1640, where he joined the painters' guild and in 1656 helped found the painters' confraternity *Pictura*. He moved to Delft in 1657 and returned to his native town in 1663. From 1669 until 1674 he lived in Amsterdam. From there he moved to Alkmaar and then to Gouda, where he remained from 1675 to 1677. In 1678 he settled in Overschie, where he spent the rest of his life. Van Beyeren, who perhaps studied with his father-in-law, the fish painter Pieter de Putter, painted all types of still lifes, but is best known for those with fish.

This freely brushed, monochromatic seascape, formerly attributed to Jan van Goyen, whose monogram was once painted over that of Van Beyeren,[2] demonstrates Van Beyeren's debt to the better-known marine painter. As in all his seascapes, Van Beyeren strives for great movement; yet here the individual waves are given the appearance of solid forms, which results in a static quality and suggests the artist's greater strength as a still-life painter. Van Beyeren's rather limited experience in marine painting may also explain the awkward way in which the man in the rowboat handles the oars as well as the unconvincing relationship between the water and the two boats in the foreground.

The real beauty of this seascape lies in the sky, which makes up the greater part of the composition. Unlike the water, the vigorously painted clouds convey an obvious sense of movement. To suggest the mood of an overcast day at sea, Van Beyeren uses an extremely limited palette of silvery grays and grayish greens, relieved by only a few touches of salmon on the flags and on the figures in the boats.

Van Beyeren may have intended a specific town with the briefly sketched buildings in the left distance (fig. 3a). The same view appears in a closely

3a Detail of *Rough Sea*

3b Abraham van Beyeren, *Rough Sea with View of a Town*, oil on canvas, 69.8 x 112 cm. Budapest, Szépmüvészeti Muzeum

related composition in Budapest (fig. 3b). In both paintings, the church depicted resembles that of the South Holland town Den Briel; however, not all of the buildings to the right of the church agree with those found on contemporary views and plans of that town, suggesting that the artist probably took liberties in both representations.

1 The label describes the painting as a view of the Hollandsch Diep, an estuary in South Holland.

2 The false Van Goyen monogram, remains of which can still be seen, is cited in both the Grigsby Sale (1912) and the Anderson Sale (1916).

Jan de Bray

Haarlem ca. 1625-27 – 1697 Haarlem

4

The Penitent Magdalen

Oil on cradled panel, 72.6 x 56.2 cm

Signed and dated at lower center on crucifix: JDBray/167(?)/25

Provenance: Galerie Marcus, Paris, 1972 (as by Pieter de Grebber); private collection.

Exhibition: *Dutch Religious Art of the Seventeenth Century*, The Yale University Art Gallery, New Haven, Conn., 21 January–16 March 1975, no. 9.

Jan de Bray was the eldest son and probably the pupil of painter and architect Salomon de Bray. He spent most of his life in his native city, where he frequently held office in the painters' guild. After a two-year stay in Amsterdam around 1686 to 1688, he returned to Haarlem, where he declared bankruptcy in 1689. Chiefly active as a portrait artist, De Bray also painted some biblical, mythological, and genre subjects.

The Magdalen was one of the most popular saints in Renaissance and Baroque art.[1] She is shown here with almost all of her major attributes. The skull and crucifix suggest the saint's contemplation of eternal life after death. The open book implies her meditative life, and the whip, which lies on top of the book, symbolizes her penitence.

The saint's long, flowing hair is also a symbol of her penitence. According to the biblical account (Luke 7:37, 38), the Magdalen expressed her love for Christ by washing his feet with her tears and wiping them with her hair. The container with a perforated top, partially visible behind the saint's left arm, is an ointment jar, which refers not only to the scene in which the Magdalen both washed and annointed the feet of Christ, but also the scene at the sepulcher, after the Crucifixion, when the Magdalen and two other women brought sweet spices to annoint the body of Christ (Mark 16:1).

Basically a figure painter, De Bray reduces the background to a minimum. A large dark area of brown and a few pieces of vine silhouetted against a small section of sky suggest the interior of a cave, where, according to legend, the Magdalen spent her later life as a hermit.[2]

With all its iconographic trappings, De Bray's devotional representation has strong Catholic overtones. Probably a Roman Catholic himself,[3] De Bray received numerous commissions from members of that religion throughout

25

23

his career. That this New Testament subject may also have been commissioned by a Catholic seems a strong possibility.

The saint's specific features and direct eye contact with the viewer give the appearance of a portrait. At this time, it was not uncommon to find contemporary persons being portrayed as religious, historical, or mythological figures. In fact, De Bray himself is known to have painted such portraits.[4] In this case, the woman may be assuming the role of her patron saint.[5]

Except for the small passage of blue sky and the green vines at the entrance to the cave, De Bray's painting is made up entirely of tones of red, white, and brown. The saint's bright red outer garment provides the keynote of color and harmonizes with her auburn hair and intense red lips. Small touches of deep crimson on the crucifix call attention to Christ's wounds.

One cannot be absolutely certain of the last digit of the date on the painting, but it may be read as 1670. Stylistically the work belongs to the artist's late period, when he abandoned the more detailed style of the preceding decades for a broader and looser type of brushwork, while still maintaining a strong plastic quality.

1 A De Bray drawing of the repentant Magdalen shown in half length was recorded in two earlier Amsterdam sales: 4 March 1765, no. 32 and 19 May 1925, no. 103. A vertical composition of similar proportions (290 x 197 mm), this black chalk drawing, the present whereabouts of which is unknown, may be a preparatory work for the painting. De Bray often made preparatory drawings for his paintings; see G. W. von Moltke, "Jan de Bray," *Marburger Jahrbuch für Kunstwissenschaft* 11–13 (1938/39): 421–523.

2 The story of the Magdalen's pilgrimage to Sainte-Baume, France, where she spent thirty years in fasting and penance, comes from the 13th-century *Golden Legend* and is based on much earlier legends about another female penitent, Mary of Egypt.

3 For a discussion of De Bray's faith, see F. W. Robinson, *"The Banquet of Anthony and Cleopatra by Jan de Bray," The Currier Gallery of Art Bulletin* (October–December 1969), n. 18.

4 For a discussion of this practice and examples by De Bray, see Robinson, *"The Banquet."*

5 It is tempting to think that the woman represented may be the artist's third wife, Victoria Stalpert van der Wiele, whose second name was Maria Magdalena. De Bray married his third wife on 23 January 1678 (his second wife died on 10 May 1673). She was from a well-known Roman Catholic family then living in The Hague. A search in the city archives at The Hague has not uncovered any birth record for her; however, she does seem to be the same Victoria Magdalena Stalpert van der Wiele who in a notorial protocol dated 1 November 1655 (N.A. 306, folio 364 and 344vo) is recorded as twelve years of age, which would make the year of her birth 1643. She died on 25 April 1680. I am grateful to J. W. M. Klomp of the Gemeentearchief, The Hague, for conducting the archival search and informing me about the 1655 document.

Pieter Claesz.

Burgsteinfurt 1597/8 – 1661 Haarlem

5

Still Life

Oil on panel, 66.7 x 71.1 cm

Signed and dated on left plate: PC 1643.

Provenance: F. Lorenz, Massapequa Park, N.Y.; private collection.

Exhibitions: Smith College Museum of Art, Northampton, Mass., 1–27 October 1968, no. 18; Sterling and Francine Clark Art Institute, Williamstown, Mass., Summer 1977.

Literature: J. S. Held and D. Posner, *17th and 18th Century Art* (New York: H. N. Abrams, 1971), p. 230, fig. 237.

Born in Westphalia of Dutch parents, Claesz. was living in Haarlem by 1617. There he appears to have spent the rest of his life specializing in still lifes. With Willem Claesz. Heda, he pioneered in the painting of breakfast still lifes in monochromatic tones. His son Nicolaes, who adopted the name Berchem, became one of the Netherlands's most important and successful painters of the Italianate landscape.

Characteristic of Claesz.'s late style, this vigorously painted still life shows the artist moving away from the monochromatic palette of his earlier years and focusing more on local color, which here includes the primary hues: the yellow of the lemon, the red of the ham, and the blue of the mustard pot. His modeling also takes on greater latitude, ranging from the detailed rendering of the overturned tazza to the impressionistic treatment of the table cloth at the back left.

Through his skillful arrangement, Claesz. imparts a pleasing unity to a wide variety of shapes and textures, all contained within a relatively limited amount of space. By incorporating a strong diagonal of light against the back wall, he counterbalances the opposing movement created by the objects themselves.

Cornelis Cornelisz. van Haarlem

Haarlem 1562 – 1683 Haarlem

6

Young Man Holding a Pen

Oil on beveled panel, 54.5 x 40.8 cm

Inscribed upper right: ÆTAT. 21/A° 1625

Verso: Label from Royal Academy Exhibition, 1910. Stenciled number *8506S*. Several illegible paper labels.

Provenance: Edward Speyer, Ridgehurst, Shenley, Herts (as by Joos van Cleve); sale, Mrs. Edward Speyer, Christie's, London, 27 June 1930, no. 97 (as by C. van Haarlem); sale, Christie's, London, 22 July 1935, no. 58; sale, Christie's, London, 26 June 1936, no. 75; sale, Christie's, London, 10 December 1937, no. 123; sale, Christie's, London, 22 July 1938, no. 58; sale, Louis Joseph Auction Gallery, Boston; private collection.[1]

Exhibition: Royal Academy Winter Exhibition, Burlington House, London, 1910, no. 102 (as by Joos van Cleve, lent by Edward Speyer).

Cornelis Cornelisz., known as Cornelis van Haarlem, is said to have first studied in his home town with Pieter Pietersz. and later with Gillis Congnent at Antwerp. By 1583 he was back in Haarlem, where, together with Karel van Mander and Hendrick Goltzius, he established an academy, a loose organization of artists who chose "to study from life." A leading figure in the final phase of Dutch Mannerism, Cornelis painted mainly portraits and religious and mythological subjects. In the 1590s he abandonned the Mannerist style for a mild classicism, which he maintained throughout the rest of his career.

The faint inscription at the upper right of this portrait gives the young man's age as twenty-one. His serious expression combined with the pen and paper suggest a studious individual. Dressed in a sober but stylish costume, he assumes a rather sophisticated pose, with one hand resting on his hip and the other on the table in front of him.

The simplified composition and thin application of paint are all characteristic of Cornelis's late style; yet even here one still finds traces of Mannerism. For example, the young man's left arm, which at first glance appears relaxed, is actually pulled toward the picture plane in an unnatural fashion in order to create a pleasing silhouette, which in turn is heightened by the soft lighting from behind. This emphasis on contours can also be seen in the hand holding the pen, where subtle chiaroscuro and careful positioning of the hand and individual fingers again stress outline over three-dimensional form.

---

1 I am grateful to Dr. P. J. J. van Thiel for information on the painting's provenance.

Benjamin Gerritsz. Cuyp

Dordrecht 1612 – 1652 Dordrecht

7

Fisherfolk and Mounted Figures on the Beach

Oil on canvas, 92 x 144 cm

Signed twice, lower left (1) and on tower at upper right (2): cuÿp, cuyp

Provenance: The Right Honorable The Viscount Chilston; sale, Christie's, London, 28 October 1966, no. 88; private collection.

Benjamin Cuyp was the stepbrother and pupil of Jacob Gerritsz. Cuyp and the uncle of the well-known landscape painter Aelbert Cuyp. In 1631 he entered the painters' guild at Dordrecht, where he appears to have spent most of his life. His oeuvre consists mainly of biblical subjects and scenes of military and peasant life.

In this painting the dramatic sweep of the clouds combined with the artist's coarse brushwork conveys the blustery atmosphere of a windy day on the coast. Counterbalancing the great lateral movement of the sky are three distinct areas of spotlighting along the beach, which like giant stepping stones carry the viewer from the immediate foreground past the various groups of figures to the sea.

Cuyp painted at least a dozen coastal scenes similar to this one. Several of these works include a view of Scheveningen, the fishing town near The Hague. Here Scheveningen is suggested by the light tower on the dune at the right. This work appears to date around 1643,[1] the year that Cuyp was mentioned as living in The Hague.[2]

---

1 The only known dated coastal scene by Cuyp, a view near Egmond aan Zee, located north of The Hague, was painted in 1643 (oil on panel, 43.2 x 62.2 cm; sold by Sotheby's, London, 23 June 1937, no. 42) (Photo: Witt Library, Courtauld Institute, University of London, London [hereafter cited as Witt]).

2 See G. H. Veth, "Aelbert Cuyp, Jacob Gerritsz Cuyp en Benjamin Cuyp," *Oud-Holland* 2 (1884): 253, n. 48.

---

1   2

Dutch School

8

Portrait of a Woman

Oil on canvas, 111.1 x 84.4 cm

Inscribed upper right: *Atatis 53 | A° dnī 1613 –*

Verso: Two labels with numbers *688/3* and *9894/e3*. Old, illegible seal in red wax.

Provenance: Dealer, Doll and Richards, Boston; private collection.

An inscription at the upper right gives the sitter's age as fifty-three and the date of the painting as 1613. Although this portrait cannot be connected with any of the known masters working at this time, the linear quality of the face suggests the Amsterdam or Delft School. The pose derives from the late sixteenth century and was used by Van der Voort and Miereveld, among others. In comparison with the face, the hands are rather soft and exhibit a slightly different palette, suggesting that the painting may be the work of more than one artist, a practice not uncommon among portrait painters of this period.

Rather conservatively dressed, the middle-aged woman wears a soft, white collar and cap, which in style date from the late sixteenth century. The rest of her costume consists of a black silk dress with velvet sleeves and a long, fur-lined, sleeveless coat (*vlieger*) with elaborate fur-trimmed shoulder pieces (*wieljes*). The costume, with its various textures, is skillfully rendered. By contrast, the chair, like the hands, exhibits a certain weakness in the modeling.

The placement of the woman suggests that this painting was the pendant to a male portrait, which according to tradition would have hung to the left. This suggestion is supported by the location of the inscription: placed to the right of the woman's head, it would not interfere with the space between the two sitters.

Ætatis 53
A° dnī 1613 –

Johannes Hannot
Leiden 1633 – 1685 Leiden

9

Still Life with Lobster
Oil on canvas, 83.8 x 72 cm

Signed lower left: J Hannot fc.

Provenance: Dealer, J. & S. Goldschmidt, Amsterdam, 1923; private collection.

The son of a tailor who came from the southern Netherlands, Johannes Hannot appears to have spent his entire life in Leiden, where he was both wine merchant and painter.[1] An active member in the guilds of both professions,[2] he is perhaps best known to art historians for the fact that in 1665 a room in his home on the Breestraat (No. 117) was used for an exhibition of paintings by Gerrit Dou.[3] Hannot, who specialized in fruit still lifes, shows the influence of the Leiden artist Jan Davidsz. de Heem.

This painting must be considered the largest and most ambitious of Hannot's known works.[4] Here the artist creates a *trompe l'oeil* effect by painting in not only the simple wood molding used to frame the picture, but also the curtain that would have hung in front of it for protection.[5] To add to the illusion, Hannot shows the white napkin of the still life overlapping the wood frame at the bottom. Such illusionistic devices were popular among Leiden artists and were especially promoted by the master Dou.[6]

In the tradition of De Heem, Hannot strives for an image of abundance through a rich combination of fruits, wines, a boiled lobster, and several elegant vessels. Except for the lemon, all of the fruits are shown with their leaves, which suggests they were grown in the Netherlands, possibly in the famous botanical gardens of Leiden University. Since the fruits represented appeared at different times of the year, one must assume that Hannot, like other still-life artists, took liberties with his juxtapositions. The orange, the rarest of the fruits depicted, is given a prominent position on top of the silver standing salt,[7] which dates from the 1650s or 1660s.[8] The blue and white porcelain bowl next to the salt is Chinese of the Wan Li period (1572–1619) and contains cultivated strawberries. In the background, as if in reference to the artist's other profession, stand a large, stemmed goblet of white wine and a tall "flute" glass of red wine.

To imitate the various textures of the objects, Hannot takes advantage of numerous painting techniques. He uses a series of glazes to produce the luminous sheen on the stiff, satin curtain. To capture the soft surface of the peaches, he scumbles the paint, and to suggest the pitted texture of the lemon peel, he applies thick paint in a stippled fashion.

9a Console from façade of town hall, Leiden, 1597 (Photo: courtesy J. J. Terwen)

The brilliant green curtain serves to break up an essentially symmetrical arrangement dominated by the multi-colored stone niche. The entire left side of the niche shows a pronounced pentimento, which occurs when an earlier design, painted over by the artist, becomes visible as the upper layers of paint acquire translucency with age. The pentimento shows the artist originally painted the left side of the niche as a fluted post on a stepped base. The curious head in relief at the top appears also to have been part of the earlier design. Masks like this one are common in Mannerist architecture, although they usually take the form of a console or bracket. Hannot's head in relief may have been inspired by the many similar Mannerist heads on the Leiden town hall, located just across the street from his residence. One of these heads, which faced the artist's house, appears in figure 9a.

Hannot's rusticated stonework, characterized by a diamond-head design, is actually an exterior type of architecture. This same Flemish-Mannerist style can again be found on the facade of the Leiden town hall, in particular on the niches and windows. One of these units, like that found in figure 9b, would have been a convenient source for Hannot's architectural design.[9]

1 I am grateful to Leiden archivist P. J. M. de Baar for uncovering new documents on Hannot, including his birth and death records. Hannot's father, Michiel, who came from around Liège, became a citizen of Leiden in 1629. Generally referred to in documents as a wine merchant, Johannes Hannot was apparently successful at this trade, for among his clientele were the magistrates at the town hall and the wardens of Leiden's three main churches.

2 At the time of his death, Hannot was recorded as dean of the wine guild. Inscribed in the painters' guild in 1653, he served as its dean in 1664, 1670, 1677, and 1681. Were it not for his death, Hannot also would have been dean in 1685 ("Dienstboek," Gemeentearchief, Leiden).

3 On 18 September 1665, Dou's patron, Johan de Bye, rented a room from Hannot to exhibit 29 of the master's works. See W. Martin, *Gerard Dou*, trans. Clara Bell (London: G. Bell and Sons, 1908), p. 66ff.

4 Documented works by Hannot are rare. His signed still lifes are found in Amsterdam, Rijksmuseum; Bonn, Rheinisches Landesmuseum; Kassel, Staatliche Gemäldegalerie; Oxford, Ashmolean Museum (Ward Bequest); and Zurich, Ruzicka Foundation. Of these paintings, the only dated works are at Amsterdam (1668) and Bonn (1654).

5 The original composition included more of the frame and curtain than is shown here. At the time the painting was lined, probably in the 19th century, the tacking edge and part of the painted surface were cut off on all four sides. When the painting was restretched, part of the design was folded over the stretcher to serve as the new tacking edge.

6 In fact, one of the Dou paintings exhibited in Hannot's house was a *vanitas* still life (now in Dresden, Gemäldegalerie, no. 1708), in which the objects are also displayed in a gray stone niche with a green curtain painted on the right. See Martin, *Dou*, pp. 68–69 and pl. 33.

7 The prominently placed orange may refer to the House of Orange as it often does in portraits of the period. Out of power from 1650–72, during the De Witt régime, the House of Orange resumed its rule in June 1672.

8 The overall design of the standing salt parallels that of others produced in Leiden at this time, such as the set of four made in 1655 for the city council by the Leiden silversmith Barend Gast;

9b Detail from façade of town hall, Leiden, 1597 (Photo: courtesy J. J. Terwen)

see *Leids Zilver*, exh. cat. (Leiden: Stedelijk Museum de Lakenhal, 1977), p. 44, no. 20, fig. 20. For further information on the standing salt, see J. R. ter Molen, *Zout op tafel: de geschiedenis van het zoutvat*, exh. cat. (Rotterdam: Museum Boymans-van Beuningen, 1976).

9 I would like to thank Professor J. J. Terwen of the University of Leiden for information on the Leiden town hall as well as for photos of the architectural details.

Abraham Hondius

Rotterdam ca. 1625–30 – 1695 London

10

Rest on the Hunt

Oil on canvas, 49 x 64.8 cm

Signed and dated on ruin, lower right: Abraham Hondius / 1665

Provenance: Private collection.

Hondius worked in his home town, Rotterdam, until 1659, when he went to live in Amsterdam. In 1666 he left the Netherlands and spent the rest of his life in London. It is not known with whom Hondius studied, but his many depictions of hunting scenes and fighting animals show the influence of the Antwerp painters Jan Fyt and Frans Snyders. Also included in Hondius's oeuvre are portraits and religious, mythological, and allegorical subjects.

Painted while Hondius was still in Amsterdam, this work depicts one of the quieter moments of the hunt; but typical of Hondius, the subject is treated with great flair and drama. His characteristically spirited brushwork conveys the joie de vivre of two amorous young hunters. Adding to the excitement are the strong spotlighting and brilliant display of color, from the exotic pink and turquoise sky to the rich play of complementaries on the fashionable costumes. A true colorist, Hondius even infuses his grays with a variety of hues, as seen in the antique ruin in the background.

An underlying baroque construction draws all attention to the young couple. The strong contrast between the ivory complexion of the female and the ruddy face of the man is but one of the many rich juxtapositions of color and value found throughout. The woman, dressed in the height of fashion from head to toe, wears in her hair some pearls and a bunch of rose-colored feathers. Her attractive, red silk dress with puff sleeves is pulled up over her knees, exposing a dark green satin underdress. A pair of matching pink bows sets off her extremely elongated, white high-heeled shoes. In her left hand she holds a large yellow plume, which like the feathers in her hair and her décolleté costume suggests a rather licentious nature.[1]

The young man wears a pair of lavendar gray breeches and a gold silk doublet with slashed sleeves and a lining of stunning pink. One of his highly fashionable hunting boots is pulled down to reveal two silk stockings, a yellow one over a gold. Equally well attired are the couple's two pages, one of whom, dressed in turquoise and salmon, pours the woman some wine, while the other, in pink and white, tends the horses.

10a Detail of *Rest on the Hunt*

10b Detail of *Rest on the Hunt*

40

10c Detail of *Rest on the Hunt*

Included in the scene are several dogs, Hondius's favorite subject and, inter-estingly, a play on his own last name. The elegant white greyhound, strongly spotlighted at the woman's right, plays an important role in the overall design. His sleek profile, like an arrow, draws the viewer's attention to the principal figures. In the shadow behind him appears the head of another greyhound, whose fiery, marble-shaped eyes—a hallmark of Hondius's ani-mals—glow on his dark brown face. Off to the right a Brittany spaniel laps water from a small pool, which also serves to cool a second flask of wine.

Next to the Brittany spaniel lies a piece of ruin with two heads carved in relief at right angles to each other (fig. 10a). Antique ruins, like the Corin-thian structure in the background and the piece of column in the left fore-ground, were a favorite of Hondius; yet, in spite of the many times he includes them in his paintings, he is not known to have ever traveled to Italy. Hondius's interest in this area may well have been encouraged by his father, who was a stone mason.

As if to indicate the success of the day, the hunter holds in his left hand a long rifle and dead bittern. An owl perched on a small cage appears at the far right (fig. 10b).[2] The owl was used to attract small birds, which the hunter would then kill or capture.[3] As proof of the success of this technique, a large string of dead birds hangs beneath the cage, while several more fly about inside. Judging from their red heads, black wings, and ochre breasts, these small birds appear to be finches.[4] Those inside the cage would probably have been kept as songsters and the others were to be eaten. In the background, seen against the mountainous terrain, are two more figures who carry on the hunt (fig. 10c). One rides a white horse, while the other, on foot, is accom-panied by a dog.

In Hondius's painting the theme of the hunt takes on erotic connotations. As demonstrated by De Jongh, the Dutch word for fowling (*vogelen*) was a

HABET VENENVM SVVM BLANDA ORATIO.

XXV.

10d Emblem XXV ("sweet talk has its poison") from Jacob Cats's *Maechden-plicht ofte ampt der ionck-vrovwen, . . .* , Middelburg: H. vander Hellen, 1618, p. 51 (Photo: The Newberry Library, Chicago)

popular expression during the seventeenth century for sexual intercourse.[5] Surely the double meaning would not have gone unnoticed in this painting in which the man holds a large bird in one hand and with the other grasps the voluptuous young woman.

Given the hunter's suave and worldly appearance, a moralist of the day would have offered the enchanted female partner a word of advice. "Sweet talk has its poison" was the popular warning for the woman who might be led astray by the flattering speeches of her lover. It is not surprising that for his illustration of this same advice, the moralist Jacob Cats chose none other than the theme of bird hunting. Cats's emblem (fig. 10d) shows a man capturing small birds using a snapnet and a lure in the form of a caged song bird; significantly, he is assisted by Cupid.

Successful in capturing birds, Hondius's hunter appears to be enjoying equal success in winning the heart of the young woman. The caged finches echo the main subject and serve as a reminder of love's power. A well-known symbol of love, the bird cage might well summarize the theme of Hondius's painting, for just as the cage imprisons the bird, so love imprisons men and women.[6]

---

1 For the association between feathers and unchastity, see E. de Jongh et al., *Tot lering en vermaak*, exh. cat. (Amsterdam: Rijksmuseum, 1976), pp. 58–61 (hereafter cited as *Tot lering en vermaak*).

2 The owl on a perch-cage appears in other paintings by Hondius: *A Hawking Party*, also dated 1665, Fitzwilliam Museum, Cambridge (cat. 1960, no. 356), and a painting last recorded in the Linz collection, no. 2730 (Photo: Rijksbureau voor Kunsthistorische Documentatie, The Hague [hereafter cited as RKD]).

3 See F. von Pfannenberg, *Die Hüttenjagd mit dem Uhu* (Neumann, Neudamm, 1910). I am grateful to G. F. Mees of the Rijksmuseum van Natuurlijke Historie, Leiden, for his comments on the birds in this painting.

4 See the two still lifes by Vonck, p. 121.

5 See E. de Jongh, "Erotica in vogelperspectief. De dubbelzinnigheid van een reeks 17de eeuwse genrevoorstellingen," *Simiolus* 3 (1968/69): 22–74.

6 The encaged bird can also represent maidenhood, with the escape of the bird standing for the loss of virginity; see p. 57.

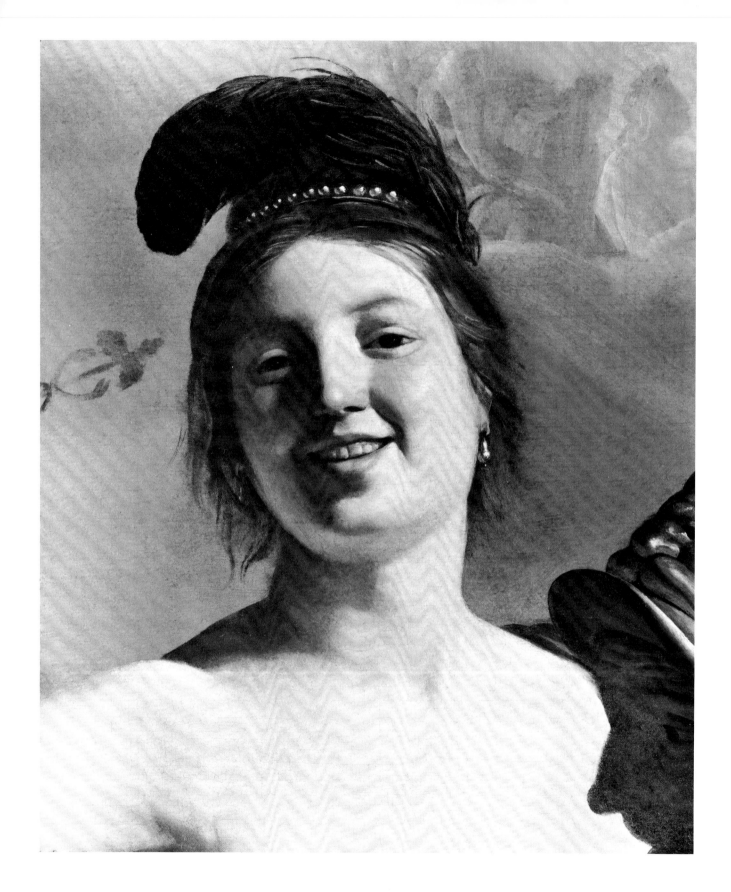

Gerrit van Honthorst

Utrecht 1590 – 1656 Utrecht

11

Head of a Smiling Girl

Oil on canvas, 42.5 x 35.1 cm

Verso: Label with number *182*. Tape with number *580*.

Provenance: Capt. F. P. Haines; sale, Christie's, London, 16 December 1927, no. 107 (as by Judith Leyster); dealer, Frank T. Sabin, Ltd., London; sale, Sir Frank Newsom-Smith and others, Christie's, London, 26 January 1951, no. 137 (as by Judith Leyster); Arcade Gallery, London, 1953/54; David M. Koetser Gallery, Zurich, 1966; private collection.

Exhibitions: *Mannerist and Baroque Pictures at the Arcade Gallery*, Arcade Gallery, London, 18 November–24 December 1953, no. 11; Sterling and Francine Clark Art Institute, Williamstown, Mass., Summer 1977.

Literature: J. R. Judson, *Gerrit van Honthorst* (The Hague: M. Nijhoff, 1959), p. 250, no. 200.

11a *Head of a Smiling Girl*, before cleaning

After studying with Abraham Bloemaert in Utrecht, Honthorst went to Rome where he is thought to have arrived around 1610 to 1612. There he enjoyed Italian patronage while studying the works of Caravaggio and the Carracci. Mastering Caravaggio's dramatic use of light, Honthorst painted many nocturnal scenes for which he soon became known as "Gherardo delle Notti." In 1620 Honthorst returned to Utrecht, where he became an important teacher and one of the main conveyers of the Caravaggesque tradition. He also introduced to the Netherlands the Italian tradition of illusionistic ceiling painting. After his return to the North, Honthorst painted fewer religious subjects and instead concentrated on portraits and classical, allegorical, and genre subjects. His fame as a painter soon spread, winning him royal commissions in England, Denmark, and the Netherlands.

When this painting was acquired by its present owner, much of the original design had been painted over (fig. 11a). Removal of these later additions revealed that the yellow dress worn by the woman was used to conceal a nude figure. The cleaning also uncovered part of the head of a man (as verified by traces of a mustache) with a helmet, as well as several less obvious forms in the golden-colored background. These forms include, at the upper right, two figures facing to the right and seated in what appear to be clouds, and, just to the left of the woman's head, the upper half of a caduceus. A well-known attribute of the god Mercury, the caduceus consists of a staff with a pair of wings and two intertwined serpents.

With these additional elements now visible, it is clear that the work is a fragment of a much larger composition. Although the original painting appears to have been a major work, and possibly a commission, there are no known records of it. As originally suggested by Judson, the work seems to date from around 1623.[1] Here, as in other paintings from Honthorst's early post-Italian period, the forms are still soft and fleshy and the colors clear and strong.

The woman represented is a typical Honthorst figure with a full face and a smile showing both teeth and gums. Part of a blue drape appears on her left shoulder. She wears pearl earrings and in her hair is a band of pearls along

11b Gerrit van Honthorst, *Mars and Venus,* pen, brown wash, and white highlights on brownish paper, 208 x 310 mm. Munich, Staatliche Graphische Sammlung

with a brilliant blue feather, which like the blue drapery forms a pleasing accent to the intense yellow orange background. During the seventeenth century, women often wore feathers in their hair (see preceding entry), a fashion that appears in many of Honthorst's genre scenes. This woman, however, does not appear to represent a contemporary figure, for she is placed next to a man whose anthropomorphic helmet suggests an allegorical or historical personage. The same type of armor can be found in other works by Honthorst, including his drawing of Mars and Venus (fig. 11b) in which Mars's helmet, footgear, and sword hilt are all decorated with similar mask-like designs.[2]

A close examination of the two figures at the upper right shows that the larger one holds a viol and what may be a bow, while the other, seated on a slightly lower level, holds what appears to be a lyre.[3] The caduceus at the left side of the picture, judging from its relative size, appears to be a considerable distance in front of the two celestial musicians and somewhat behind the two life-sized figures in the foreground. The fragmentary state of the painting makes it difficult to establish the exact relationship between the foreground figures and the figurative elements in the background. The monochromatic tones of the background suggest the possibility of a flat surface, such as a tapestry or wall painting, and yet the cool daylight on the smiling girl seems to imply an exterior scene. Nevertheless, whether the background is two-dimensional or three-dimensional, one can assume from its intense coloring and relative clarity that it was intended to add to the meaning of the man and woman in the foreground.

It is interesting to speculate on which subject Honthorst intended in this painting. One possibility is an allegory on Peace and War with the helmeted figure representing Mars and the female figure representing Peace or Venus. The nudity and pearls specifically suggest Venus. Shown in a frontal position and fully illuminated, the smiling female takes a triumphant position over the man, who, by contrast, appears in shadow and wears a frown. The caduceus, itself a symbol of peace, suggests the presence of Mercury, who would serve as the messenger carrying the news of peace back to the gods, represented by the celestial figures at the upper right. With their musical instruments, these same figures may also symbolize the harmony brought about by Peace.

Whether Honthorst intended an allegory on Peace and War is at this point impossible to verify. Adding to the problem of determing the subject is the fact that in addition to well-known Baroque themes, Honthorst painted many less common and even some very obscure subjects, such as Lais and Xenocrates.[4] Also included in his oeuvre are paintings whose subjects are still open to interpretation.[5] Therefore, until additional information is uncovered, such as a preparatory drawing or a related engraving or document, one can only speculate on the full meaning of this important and intriguing fragment.

---

1 Judson, *Honthorst*, p. 250, no. 200, compared *Head of a Smiling Girl* to the lute player in Honthorst's *Allegory* dated 1623, in the Bayerische Staatsgemäldesammlungen, Munich. At the time of Judson's writing, *Head of a Smiling Girl* was still painted over as in figure 11a.

2 Judson dates the drawing around 1621 (ibid., p. 257, no. 223). The soldiers in Honthorst's contemporary scenes do not wear this type of helmet, but instead the fancy, plumed caps so characteristic of the Caravaggisti.

3 Honthorst included celestial musicians in two religious paintings both dated 1618: *St. Paul Caught up into the Third Heaven*, S. Maria della Vittoria, Rome, and *Madonna and Child with Saints Francis and Bonaventura and Princess Colonna-Gonzaga*, Church of the Capuchins, Albano. Both paintings are illustrated in Judson, *Honthorst*, pls. 7, 8.

4 Honthorst's *Lais and Xenocrates* is dated 1623. See Judson, *Honthorst*, p. 194, no. 103, pl. 31.

5 One example is Honthorst's *Allegory* (see n. 1 above), discussed and illustrated by Judson, *Honthorst*, pp. 205–8, pl. 27. For the range of Honthorst's subjects, see Judson's catalogue raisonné.

Adrian van der Kabel

Rijswijk 1631 – 1705 Lyons

12

Beach Scene

Oil on beveled panel, 37.8 x 50.5 cm

Signed lower right: AVKabel or AVCabel

Provenance: Private collection, Vienna (as by Adriaen van Ostade); Paul Drey Gallery, N.Y.; private collection.

Literature: W. Bernt, *The Netherlandish Painters of the Seventeenth Century*, 3 vols. (London: Phaidon Press, 1969/70), 2: no. 605; H.-U. Beck, *Jan van Goyen 1596–1656: ein Œuvreverzeichnis*, 2 vols. (Amsterdam: Van Gendt, 1972/73) 1:58, n. 2.

Van der Kabel studied with Jan van Goyen at The Hague. At the age of twenty he left the Netherlands and traveled by way of France to Italy, where from 1660 to 1665 he was a member of the *Schildersbent,* a fraternal organization of Netherlandish artists living in Rome. From Italy he returned to France, settling in Lyons, where he remained for the rest of his life.

This painting, one of the few known works from the artist's Dutch period, reflects the strong influence of Van Goyen in its atmospheric quality, monochromatic palette, and lively drawing style. Although the painting is one of Van der Kabel's most monochromatic, even here one can observe in the basically yellow, gray, and brown tones many nuances of other hues, suggesting the extremely colorful palette that would characterize the artist's later work (see following entry).

The numerous figures, which resemble the types painted by Van Goyen, add a great deal of interest and variety to the relatively simple setting. This scene may represent the beach near Scheveningen, a favorite painting spot of Van Goyen and others. If so, the church tower in the background is a simplified version of the original structure.

Adrian van der Kabel

Rijswijk 1631 – 1705 Lyons

13

Shepherdess in an Italian Landscape

Oil on beveled panel, 23.3–23.5 x 19.2 cm

Signed lower right: AVK or AVC

Verso: The numbers *51* (stencil) and *61* (ink on paper) and two inscriptions attributing the work to Nicolaes Berchem.

Provenance: Dealer, James I. McGrath, Winchester, Mass.; private collection.

While in the Netherlands, Van der Kabel worked in the style of his teacher, Jan van Goyen, as demonstrated in the preceding painting. After leaving Holland in the early 1650s and traveling to France and Italy, he soon adopted a more romantic style in the tradition of Claude Lorrain and the Dutch painters Jan Both and Nicolaes Berchem.

Judging from Van der Kabel's drawings, many of which are dated, this picture appears to have been painted in the mid-1650s. Here, as in his earlier works, Van der Kabel continues to transfer his lively drawing style into his painting.

Incorporated into this small, southern landscape are many of the pictorial effects popularized by Berchem, to whom the work was previously attributed. Van der Kabel builds his composition around one of Berchem's favorite motifs: the shepherdess on a donkey.[1] To create the vast landscape beyond, he includes a series of overlapping hills and a distant mountain bathed in a soft, lavender haze. Van der Kabel's interest in the picturesque is evident throughout, especially in the two spindly trees, which together form a decorative screen against the extremely colorful evening sky.

---

1 The motif of a woman seated on a donkey surrounded by sheep appears in several of Van der Kabel's drawings, including one dated as early as 1651; (Sotheby Mak van Waay B.V., Amsterdam, 9 June 1975, no. 141).

Nicolaes Maes

Dordrecht 1634 – 1693 Amsterdam

14

Portrait of Helena van Heuvel

Oil on canvas, 44.3 x 34.3 cm

Signed lower right: Maes

Verso: Label inscribed *Helena van den Heuvel/Ce(z?)ari Winninx uxor.* (see fig. 14a).

Provenance: Sir G. Donaldson, London, 1890; Jules Porges, Paris; Michele Porges, N.Y.; Charles Porges, Berkeley; Denenberg Fine Arts, Boston, 1978; private collection.

Literature: E. W. Moes, *Iconographia Batava,* 2 vols. (Amsterdam: F. Muller & Co., 1897–1905), 1:418, no. 3479; HdG, 6: no. 181.

A native of Dordrecht, Maes studied in Amsterdam with Rembrandt around 1650, returning to his home town in 1653. His early works are mostly genre scenes, using the warm chiaroscuro effects of his master. Around 1660 when he began to concentrate on portraits, he changed his style, choosing the more courtly mode of the Flemish and French with its emphasis on bright colors and ornate forms. In 1673 Maes returned to Amsterdam, where he continued to paint until his death.

Helena van Heuvel (1638–1698), the daughter of a wealthy Amsterdam merchant,[1] was the second wife of Leonard Winninx (1616–1691). Winninx, also a merchant, traveled widely for the Dutch East India Company before their marriage.[2]

The identification of the sitter comes from an old inscription on the back of the painting (fig. 14a). This inscription appears to have been added by someone not very familiar with the sitter's family, for her last name is given as Van den Heuvel instead of Van Heuvel, and the first name of her husband as Cesare instead of Leonard. In fact, Cesare was the father of Leonard and spelled his last name Winnen, which the son changed to Winninx.[3] The marriage banns of Leonard Winninx and Helena van Heuvel, recorded on 27 February 1664, show the proper spelling of their names (fig. 14b).

The costume and hair style suggest that the portrait was painted around 1680, when Helena van Heuvel was forty-two years old. At the time, Maes was at the height of his career, receiving numerous portrait commissions from Amsterdam's wealthy class. His great appeal to these affluent citizens is obvious. He creates an image of status and prosperity by giving his sitter a casual but elegant pose and adorning her with rich jewelry and expensive fabrics. For a background, he chooses a romantic evening landscape, and to set off the entire work, he paints in a simple black oval frame. In spite of his

14a Inscription on back of *Portrait of Helena van Heuvel*

14b Signatures from marriage banns of Helena van Heuvel and Cesare Winninx, 27 February 1664. Amsterdam, Gemeentelijke Archiefdienst van Amsterdam

many glamorizing devices, Maes still succeeds in capturing a likeness, which includes the less attractive elements of a double chin and a certain puffiness around the eyes. These realistic details are compensated for by the artist's attention to the many rich color nuances in the woman's flesh, particularly in her face, where the play of warm and cool tones results in an extremely vibrant, life-like quality.

Maes may have painted as a pendant to this work a portrait of the sitter's husband; if he did, however, either the painting has not survived, or, as with so many portraits from the period, its sitter is no longer identified.

Portrait of Helena van Heuvel

1 Helena van Heuvel was the daughter of Nicolaes van Heuvel (1600–1646) and Eva Claes Roch (1606–1671), who lived at 48 Herengracht in *De Drie Heuvelen* ("the three hills"). See H. F. Wijnman, G. Roosegaarde de Bisschop, and I. H. van Eeghen, *Vier eeuwen Herengracht* (Amsterdam: Stadsdrukkerij van Amsterdam, 1976), pp. 410–11.

2 See W. Wijnaendts van Resandt, *De gezaghebbers der Oost-Indische Compagnie op hare buiten-comptoiren in Azië* (Amsterdam: Liebaert, 1944), pp. 279–80.

3 For information on the sitter and her family, I am grateful to S. A. C. Dudok van Heel, Gemeentelijke Archiefdienst van Amsterdam.

Frans van Mieris the Elder

Leiden 1635 – 1681 Leiden

15

Lady at Her Dressing Table

Oil on beveled panel, 31.7 x 26 cm

Verso: Pasted to the panel is the entry from an 1852 Paris sale catalogue[1] and an unidentified catalogue entry written in French.[2] Inscribed on panel in white paint *Mieris*. Several old, illegible seals in red wax.

Provenance: Comte de Turenne, Paris; sale, Comte de Turenne, Paris, 17–19 May 1852, no. 47, (as by Jan van Mieris); sale, M. H. Colnaghi, London, 19 November 1908, no. 101; William Pitt, Baltimore, 1911; Newhouse Galleries, N.Y.; private collection.

Literature: HdG, 10: no. 82d.

Exhibitions: *The Collection of Mr. and Mrs. A. W. S. Herrington of Indianapolis, Indiana,* Krannert Art Museum, Champaign, Illinois, 27 September–25 October 1964, no. 21; *The Nell Clarke Herrington Memorial Exhibition,* Art Association of Indianapolis and Herron Museum of Art, 7–28 April 1968, p. 27.

The son of a goldsmith, Frans van Mieris trained principally with the Leiden master Gerrit Dou, who referred to him as "the prince of his pupils." In 1658 Van Mieris entered the Leiden painters' guild, where he later served as an officer. After Dou, he ranks as the leading member of the Leiden school of *fijnschilders,* artists whose works are characterized by a meticulous finish. Like Dou, Van Mieris enjoyed an international reputation. He was imitated by many artists, including his two sons, Jan and Willem, and his grandson Frans van Mieris the Younger. His oeuvre, which consists mainly of portraits and genre scenes, also includes some religious, historical, and literary subjects.

Judging from the woman's costume and hair style, this work would have been painted in the last years of Van Mieris's career, when the artist returned to the *fijnschilder* technique that he had perfected in his youth. He gives full attention to the color and texture of a variety of rich materials. All of the objects on the table—the tortoise-shell jewelry box, the oriental carpet, and the mirror—appear in other paintings, both by Van Mieris and by his son Willem (1662–1747),[3] who, as both Houbraken and Van Gool imply, would have been working closely with his father at this time.[4] This painting, in fact, should be compared with a work by the son entitled *The Letter* (fig. 15a).[5] The striking similarity between these two paintings in the placement and monumental proportions of the two women suggests not only that the son was influenced by *Lady at Her Dressing Table,* but that he may even have had a hand in its creation. Particularly unusual in this painting is the young woman's face, which is a departure from the flatter, broader, and more detailed faces usually painted by the elder Van Mieris. The classical profile and generalized forms recall more the figures of Willem, in particular the idealized figures that appear in his later works.

One should also consider the nineteenth-century sale catalogue entry that assigns this painting to Frans van Mieris's other son, Jan (1660–1690).[6] Two years older than Willem, Jan appears also to have been working closely with his father at the time this picture was painted.[7] In fact, one of the rare,

15a Willem van Mieris, *The Letter*, oil on
panel, 24 x 20.5 cm. Present whereabouts
unknown (Photo: RKD)

15b Jan van Mieris, *Genre Scene*, 1680, oil on
panel, 29.5 x 23.5 cm. Present whereabouts
unknown (Photo: RKD)

15c Emblem XXI from Jacob Cats's *Proteus, ofte minne-beelden* . . . , Rotterdam: Waesberge, 1627, p. 122 (Photo: The Newberry Library, Chicago)

signed, early genre scenes by Jan (fig. 15b)[8] shows several similarities to this painting. Dated 1680, Jan's painting depicts a woman seated next to a table with an oriental carpet and looking toward a man who offers her a fruit. Behind the couple can be seen a canopied bed similar to the one that appears behind the woman in this painting. In both pictures the women are characterized by their large proportions, particularly their legs, which create similar folds in their shiny, satin gowns. Also similar in both works is the rendering of the carpet with its emphasis on the texture of the pile. One can surely suggest that Jan was also familiar with *Lady at Her Dressing Table* and may likewise have been instrumental in its creation, all of which indicates once again the strong link between all three Van Mierises during the period that marked the end of the father's career.

In this painting the woman, shown with her gown opened and her breasts partially exposed, is startled by a colorful butterfly,[9] which seems to have

15d Frans van Mieris the Elder, *The Flown Bird: Allegory on the Loss of Virginity*, 1676, oil on panel, 17.5 x 14 cm. Amsterdam, Rijksmuseum

escaped from the opened jewelry box in front of her. In the background, to the right of the canopied bed, can be seen an old woman standing in a doorway leading to a classical interior. The old woman holds a cane in one hand and with the other gives a gesture of warning. Van Mieris's imagery derives from a Dutch representation in which an elderly woman cautions a young woman about the loss of virginity, which is symbolized by a bird escaping from a cage or box,[10] as seen in Jacob Cats's *Proteus, ofte minne-*

beelden (fig. 15c). The same general theme is the subject of another painting by Frans van Mieris, as well as one by his son Willem. The father's painting (fig. 15d), dated 1676, shows a woman with a jewelry box similar to the one represented here. In that work, the woman lifts the lid of the box, thereby allowing a bird to escape. The son's painting (fig. 15e), executed in 1687, shows a woman holding a wicker bird cage, from which a bird has already escaped and is shown flying away at the upper right.

By replacing the bird with a butterfly in *Lady at Her Dressing Table,* the artist departs from the traditional interpretation of this theme, for the fleeting butterfly symbolizes not the loss of virginity, but the transitoriness of life, a well-known subject in Dutch art. This *vanitas* motif, which is reinforced by the mirror on the table, may explain the unusually idealized face of the young woman; for seen in connection with that of the withered old woman in the background, it too suggests *vanitas.*

15e Willem van Mieris, *Allegory on the Loss of Virginity,* 1687, oil on panel, 21 x 18 cm. Hamburg, Kunsthalle

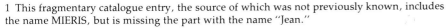

1 This fragmentary catalogue entry, the source of which was not previously known, includes the name MIERIS, but is missing the part with the name "Jean."

2 This printed entry, parts of which are missing, reads: "Une Jeune Femme assise devant sa toilette, la / (g)orge à demi découverte, vê(t)ue en satin, et qui / semble surprise de voir un papillon qui s'envole. Un / miroir, une boëte [*sic*] ouverte, et (u)ne fermée, sont placés / sur un tapis de Turquie rec(ou)vrant, a moitie, une / table de marbre. A droite, et dans le fond, une porte / ouverte par ou l'on voit une vielle femme qui semble / mécontente. Ce tableau très-agréable est aussi d . . . / couleur brillante, et d'une belle harmonie. Ha(uteur) / 12 p., largeur 10 p. Sur bois."

3 The same jewelry box can be seen in Willem van Mieris's Dresden painting dated 1709. The oriental carpet was also used in the *Tric-Trac Players,* a work signed *F. van Mieris* and dated 1680 (formerly Newhouse Galleries, N.Y.). The mirror, with its ornate gold frame, which includes a standing female figure on the side, appears in two paintings by Willem van Mieris: *The Letter* (fig. 15a) and *The Sick Young Woman,* dated 1709 (Petit Sale, Paris, 29 May 1913, no. 47). In both works by the son, the mirror is accompanied by a matching brush. In *The Sick Young Woman,* the mirror is shown from the front. Pentimento shows that in *Lady at Her Dressing Table* the mirror was originally taller and the support on the back was longer and at a slightly different angle. These changes, made by the artist, are confirmed by infrared photography.

4 A. Houbraken, *De groote schouburgh der Nederlantsche konstschilders en schilderessen . . . ,* 3 vols. (Amsterdam: A. Houbraken, 1718–21), 3:12 (hereafter cited as Houbraken); J. van Gool, *De nieuwe schouburgh der Nederlantsche kunstschilders en schilderessen . . . ,* 2 vols. (The Hague: J. van Gool, 1750/51), 1: 191.

5 HdG, 10:no. 284. This painting was last recorded in the Charpentier Sale, Paris, 5 December 1951, no. 38.

6 This catalogue entry is pasted to the back of the painting (see n. 1 above).

7 J. van Gool, *Schouburgh,* 2:442 refers to the father's influence on the son.

8 This work, which is similar in size to the work attributed to the father, was last recorded in a Lepke sale, Berlin, 30 March 1925 (no. 46, pl. 24).

9 The butterfly represented here is the Peacock (*Inachis io*), formerly a common species in the Netherlands.

10 For a discussion of this theme, see *Tot lering en vermaak,* pp. 226–27.

Claes Molenaer

Haarlem (?) before 1630 – 1676 Haarlem

16

Landscape with a Bleaching Field

Oil on cradled panel, 47.1 x 63.7 cm

Signed lower right: K. Molenaer

Verso: Two Durand-Ruel labels attached to cradle, one inscribed *No. 1100 / . . . Holland;* the other, *Molenaer 1648 / paysage en Holland.*

Provenance: Durand-Ruel, N.Y.; Catholina Lambert Collection, N.Y.; Lambert Sale, 21–24 February 1916, no. 111, N.Y.; bought by A. M. Hess; private collection.

Literature: *Illustrated Catalogue of the Valuable Paintings and Sculptures by the Old and Modern Masters Forming the Famous Catholina Lambert Collection* (New York, 1916), no. 111.

16a Claes Molenaer, *Linen on the Bleaching Ground,* oil on panel, 29.5 x 37 cm (Photo: courtesy Dorotheum)

Molenaer was active in Haarlem, where he entered the Guild of St. Luke in 1651. Painting in the style of Jacob van Ruisdael, he specialized in river and canal landscapes as well as winter scenes.

One of the labels on the back of the painting gives a date of 1648. No trace of a date can be found on the painting itself; however, judging from other works by the artist,[1] a date in the late 1640s is plausible. It was during this period, early in his career, that Molenaer painted some of his finest pictures.

A variety of figures are shown washing cloth and spreading it out on the grass to be bleached.[2] Cloth bleaching, which had flourished in the Netherlands since the late Middle Ages, was a favorite subject of Molenaer. This activity, like the dunes which can be seen in the center distance, suggests a site around the artist's home town, where most of the Dutch bleaching industry was located.

Molenaer repeated this same basic composition twice. One of the other paintings (fig. 16a),[3] considerably smaller, is almost identical to this one. The other, a vertical picture (fig. 16b),[4] demonstrates the artist's ability to adapt the same design to a completely different format, mainly by consolidating the scene at the left and elongating the trees at the right.

16b Claes Molenaer, *The Bleaching Ground,* oil on panel, 51.7 x 47 cm. Kassel, Staatliche Gemäldegalerie

1 See, for example, *The Bleaching Ground near Haarlem,* dated 1647, in Leipzig.

2 A pentimento reveals that one of the figures, a woman standing in front of the cottage, was painted out by the artist.

3 This signed panel was recently sold at auction: Dorotheum, Vienna, 13 June 1978, no. 70.

4 A dendrochronological test made on the panel indicates that the work dates after 1650.

K . molenaer

Pieter de Molyn
London 1595 – 1661 Haarlem

17

Landscape with Travelers and a Church

Oil on panel, 40.5 x 60.9 cm

Signed and dated lower left: PMolÿn/1648

Verso: Fragments of a Baden newspaper with the date 1854. Label inscribed *16. Peter Molyn.* Old, illegible seal in red wax.

Provenance: Private collection.

Born in London of Flemish parents, Molyn emigrated to Holland, where in 1616 he joined the Guild of St. Luke at Haarlem. There he spent most of his life. First influenced by Mannerist artists like Abraham Bloemaert, he was soon attracted to the realistic landscapes of Esias van de Velde. Together with Salomon van Ruysdael and Jan van Goyen, Molyn made significant contributions to landscape painting during the late 1620s. He was also active as printmaker and draughtsman.

The brilliant blue sky, Italianate church, and classical ruins all associate this scene with Italy. Although antique architecture appears in works painted throughout Molyn's career,[1] it is not known whether he ever traveled south of the Alps. He may simply have referred to the works of other artists who did visit Italy.

In this very thinly painted landscape, much of the underdrawing shows through,[2] revealing that the initial composition was conceived basically in terms of areas of contrasting values, as seen for example in the old church. Molyn continues the device he introduced in the late 1620s of using a strong diagonal to unite the foreground, middle distance, and background. In spite of its late date, the landscape still shows the influence of Mannerism in its extremely stylized figures.

---

1 See, for example, the drawing dated 1634 in Dresden (*Peter and John Healing a Lame Man*) and the one dated 1660 (or 1659) in the British Museum (Italian Landscape with Ruined Tower).

2 The same transparent quality can be seen in other late works by the artist, including *River Valley* (Staatliche Museen, Berlin, 1659), which W. Stechow connects with Hercules Seghers (*Dutch Landscape Painting of the Seventeenth Century*, 2nd ed., Kress Foundation Studies in the History of European Art, 1 [New York: Phaidon Press, 1968], p. 134, fig. 269).

Pieter Mulier the Elder

Haarlem ca. 1600 – 1670 Haarlem

18

Vessels on a Choppy Sea

Oil on cradled panel, 35.9 x 51.6 cm

Provenance: Nordest Gallery, Boston; private collection.

Mulier was born in Haarlem, where in 1638 he was first recorded in the local Guild of St. Luke. Among his students were Frans de Hulst and his own son, Pieter the Younger, known as Tempesta. A specialist in seascapes, Mulier worked in the tradition of Porcellis (see p. 83) and De Vlieger, concentrating mainly on the dramatic effects of the elements.

Judging from Mulier's overall development,[1] this work appears to have been painted around 1650, a date that accords with the height of the stern on the merchantman in the distance at the right. Another merchantman, with its top sail partially lowered, takes a more prominent position in the left foreground. The barge to the right of it shown with a spritsail appears to be its pilot boat. The three red-and-white flags flown by the merchantman may represent Hoorn, one of the major ports along the Zuider Zee. Although too faint to be positively identified, the town in the center distance may also refer to Hoorn.

As in many of his works, Mulier places the vessels off to the sides, which helps to suggest the vastness of the open sea and, together with the movement of clouds, implies a continuation beyond the picture plane. To offset the strong visual weight of the prominently placed vessels at the left, the artist shows all of the vessels leaning toward the right. Another small but important factor in the balance of the overall asymmetric design is the wooden barrel carefully placed in the otherwise completely empty right foreground.

---

1 See G. S. Keyes, "Pieter Mulier the Elder," *Oud Holland* 90 (1976): 230–61.

Eglon van der Neer

Amsterdam 1634(?) – 1703 Düsseldorf

19

A Mountainous Wooded Landscape

Oil on canvas, 34.9 x 43.5 cm

Signed and dated lower left: vander N . . . / 69

Provenance: Tage Wendler, Sweden; sale, London, Sotheby's, 9 May 1973, no. 138 (as by Jan Gerritsz. Stockman); private collection; sale, London, Christie's, 13 December 1974, no. 188 (as by Stockman); private collection.

Son of the landscape artist Aert van der Neer, Eglon was born in Amsterdam and, according to Houbraken,[1] was trained by his father and Jacob van Loo. After a three- or four-year stay in France, where he painted for the Dutch Governor of Orange, Van der Neer returned to Holland. There he is recorded to have lived in Amsterdam, Rotterdam, and The Hague. From 1679 to 1689 he was at Brussels, where in 1687 he received the title of court painter to Charles II of Spain. The last thirteen years of Van der Neer's life were spent as court painter to the Elector Palatine, Johann Wilhelm, at Düsseldorf. A popular artist during his lifetime, Van der Neer painted mainly landscapes and elegant interior scenes in the style of Metsu and Ter Borch.

Because of the recently discovered signature, this landscape, which was previously attributed to Jan Gerritsz. Stockman (active 1636 to 1670), can now be documented as a work by Van der Neer. None of Van der Neer's landscapes bear dates before 1690, which suggest that the numbers 6 and 9 that appear beneath the partial signature are the remains of a date in the 1690s rather than the date 1669. The work therefore would have been painted at Düsseldorf while the artist was in the service of the Elector Palatine.

Van der Neer's idealized setting with its brilliant colors and lucid forms is, like the majority of his landscapes, a complete break from his father's monochromatic and atmospheric renderings of the Dutch countryside. The son's work shows the strong influence that French and Italian landscape painters had on Dutch artists at the end of the seventeenth century. The yellow, blue, and lavender tints of the sky recall the works of Claude Lorrain, while the well-defined recession into space and the overall emphasis on order and harmony suggest the influence of Poussin. At the same time, Van der Neer's jewel-like refinement indicates a conscious return to the detailed landscapes of much earlier artists, in particular Adam Elsheimer. As with Elsheimer, the figures and animals in Van der Neer's landscapes often represent a biblical or mythological subject, a favorite being Tobias and the Angel. Here, how-

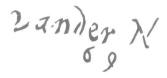

69

19a Detail of *A Mountainous Wooded Landscape*

19b Plant varieties: 1) primrose (*Primula*), 2) feverfew (*Chrysanthemum parthenium*), 3) burdock (*Arctium*), 4) grape (*Vitis vinifera*), 5) raspberry (*Rubus*), 6) wood avens (*Geum urbanum*), 7) Scotch thistle (*Onopordon acanthium*), 8) hedge bindweed (*Convolvulus sepium*), 9) carrot (*Umbelliferae*), 10) crown vetch (*Coronilla varia*), 11) daisy (*Compositae*), and 12) bedstraw (*Galium*)

ever, they are used simply to define space and enhance the pastoral setting. Close examination shows that both the figures and animals were added after the landscape was completed.

The carefully rendered plants and shrubs that Van der Neer introduces in the right foreground bear witness to his botanical interests. Houbraken reports that when Van der Neer was living in Brussels, he had a large garden in which he cultivated all kinds of plants and, by means of a small, portable shed, was able to paint them at close range.[2] This familiarity with nature is clearly demonstrated here, for one can identify at least a dozen different species (figs. 19 a,b).[3] The artist's attention to detail can be seen best, perhaps, in the raspberry, the growth of whose stem is captured in a small but brilliant passage of color—from blue gray through various shades of brown, followed by green and then yellow.

---

1 Houbraken, 3:172.

2 Ibid., 174.

3 For the identification of the plants and shrubs, I am indebted to Dr. P. W. Leenhouts of the Rijksherbarium, Leiden.

Adriaen van Ostade
Haarlem 1610 – 1685 Haarlem

20, 21

A Drinker and a Smoker

Oil on cradled panel, 19 x 17.2 cm

Signed lower right (1): A ostade

Verso: Goudstikker label, no. 674.

A Fiddler and a Drinker

Oil on cradled panel, 19 x 17.2 cm

Signed lower right (2): Av.ostade

Verso: Goudstikker label, no. 673; label from 1938 *Gedenck-Clanck* exhibition.

Provenance for both works: Collection Van Beuren; L. Nardus, N. Y.; P. A. B. Widener, Philadelphia; dealer, Hamburger Frères, Paris; J. Goudstikker Collection, Amsterdam; Newhouse Galleries, N. Y.; private collection.

Exhibitions: *A Fiddler and a Drinker* appeared in *Gedenck-Clanck*, Stedelijk Museum, Amsterdam, May 1938, no. 77 (as *Vioolspeler*, lent by Goudstikker). Both works appeared in *The Collection of Mr. and Mrs. A. W. S. Herrington of Indianapolis, Indiana*, Krannert Art Museum, Champaign, Illinois, 27 September–25 October 1964, nos. 23, 24; *The Nell Clarke Herrington Memorial Exhibition*, Art Association of Indianapolis and Herron Museum of Art, Indianapolis, 7–28 April 1968, p. 31.

Literature for both works: *Catalogue of Paintings Forming the Private Collection of P. A. B. Widener, Ashbourne—Near Philadelphia . . .*, 2 vols. (Paris: Goupil & Co., 1885–1900), 2: nos. 231, 232; HdG, 3: nos. 243, 244; J. Goudstikker, *Catalogue de la collection Goudstikker d'Amsterdam, Exposée dans les localités du schilderkundig genootschap, "Pulchri Studio" . . .* (The Hague, 1919), nos. 89, 90; idem., *Catalogue de la collection Goudstikker d'Amsterdam . . .*, 20 vols. (Haarlem: P. O. & F., 1917 [?]–31), 14: nos. 51, 52.

Ostade, the son of a weaver, spent his life in Haarlem, where he joined the Guild of St. Luke in 1634. He is reported to have been a pupil of Frans Hals at the same time as Adriaen Brouwer. It was Brouwer, however, who seems to have influenced him most in his early work. A popular and relatively well-to-do artist, Ostade produced a large number of paintings, etchings, and drawings, almost all of which are peasant genre scenes. His pupils include his younger brother, Isaack, Cornelis Dusart, and Cornelis Bega.

Identical in size, these two paintings, with their complementary designs, appear to have been made as pendants.[1] They probably date from the late 1650s, when Ostade turned to scenes with fewer figures and less activity than in his earlier works. Also pointing to this period are the subtle chiaroscuro effects, the overall warm palette, and the confinement of local color to the costumes of the figures.

1   2

73

In both paintings the figures are assigned to the lower half of the composition, leaving a relatively open space at the top, which in the work at the left is broken up by a few boards, some steps, and a railing, and in the work at the right, by a wooden wall rack containing a ceramic plate and several small objects. A pentimento in *A Smoker and a Drinker* shows that the tabletop, which was originally smaller, was extended by the artist farther to the left.[2] In the final design, the table not only supports the drinker's hand with the glass, but also helps to unite the two men. Although compositionally united, they ignore each other. Each of the figures in the two paintings is absorbed in his own world.

Ostade includes on the table in both paintings a white, clay smoking pipe. In *A Fiddler and a Drinker*, the pipe lies next to a small, metal tobacco box. Smoking, like drinking, appears often in the many genre scenes by Ostade. Then a relatively new phenomenon in the Netherlands, smoking was generally considered a social evil, as was drinking. In fact, the two, which often appear together, as in both these works, were common seventeenth-century symbols of *vanitas*. The same association was also made with musical instruments, particularly when they were used for other than religious purposes. It was in 1659, about the time these two works were painted, that the Amsterdam poet Jan van der Veen wrote: "The FIDDLE or VIOL which would better serve God is used more for vanity than for God's praise and honor."[3]

The music making, the smoking, and the drinking may also refer to three of the Five Senses, namely Hearing, Smell, and Taste, respectively. As for the other senses, Touch is suggested by the cloth on the table in the work at the left, and Sight by what may be a musical score on the table in front of the fiddler. The Five Senses was a favorite theme of Ostade, who more than once treated it as the subject of five separate works.[4] This theme, which had a long tradition in Netherlandish art, was usually seen as a reminder of the inherent dangers in worldly pleasures.

1 A painting that appears to be a copy of *A Smoker and a Drinker* was sold at Hôtel Drouot, Paris, 29–30 May 1933 (no. 44, pl. 5). A slightly larger panel (23 x 19 cm), the Paris picture seems to be the same work that was once with the dealer A. S. Drey, Munich (Photo: Witt).

2 A pentimento also appears in the other painting where the profile of the drinker's cap was changed slightly at the back.

3 "De VEDEL of FIOOL die wert God betert, meer / Gebruyckt tot ydelheyt, als tot Godts lof en eer." J. van der Veen, *Zinne-Beelden oft Adams Appel* . . . (Amsterdam, 1659), riddle 32.

4 See HdG, 3: nos. 6–27.

Egbert van der Poel

Delft 1621 – 1664 Rotterdam

22

Barnyard Scene with Two Figures and a Cart

Oil on beveled panel with balsa moisture-barrier backing, 76 x 63 cm

Provenance: Appleton Estate, Boston; private collection.

The son of a goldsmith, Van der Poel was baptized in Delft, where he entered the painters' guild in 1650. Until 1654 he concentrated on winter landscapes and canal and coastal scenes, as well as exteriors and interiors of stables and cottages. After 1654, at about which time he settled in Rotterdam, Van der Poel painted mainly scenes connected with the gunpowder explosion that destroyed a large part of his home town (12 October 1654).

One of the artist's finest early works, this painting appears to date from the late 1640s; it bears a strong connection both compositionally and stylistically to another barnyard scene by Van der Poel signed and dated 1649 (fig. 22a).[1] Influenced by Rembrandt and his followers, Van der Poel employs a concentrated light that gives his exterior scene the appearance of an interior. Featured in the strongly illuminated foreground is an eclectic still life of used and broken objects. These objects, carefully arranged in a pyramid design echoing the shape of the dilapidated building behind, offer the artist a chance to study the light as it falls on a wide variety of shapes and textures. Even the chickens are treated like inanimate objects and take on the appearance of porcelain. Given a less important role are the man and woman shown loading or unloading a cart in the middle distance. The only significant passage of intense coloring, the two figures help to emphasize the bleakness of the basically monochromatic setting.

Like Rembrandt, Van der Poel shows a preoccupation with the patina that time and use give to various objects. Dented, cracked, chipped, torn, and mended, these common objects, all carefully observed and skillfully rendered, bring the viewer as close to peasant life as the depiction of the peasants themselves.

22a Egbert van der Poel, *Barnyard Scene*, 1649, oil on panel, 75 x 62.2 cm

1 This painting recently appeared in the Leo Spik auction, Berlin, 11–12 December 1975. Its present whereabouts is unknown.

Cornelis van Poelenburgh

Utrecht 1586(?) – 1667 Utrecht

23

Psyche Received into Olympus

Oil on beveled panel, 32.7 x 40.4 cm

Verso: Printed catalogue entry with the title "festin des dieux" [1] and a typed label with the title "Die Götter des Olymp."

Provenance: Sale, Dorotheum, Vienna, 16 September 1969, no. 92; Central Picture Galleries, N.Y., 1970; private collection.

23a Detail from *Psyche Received into Olympus*

Poelenburgh, who trained with Abraham Bloemaert in Utrecht, traveled to Italy around 1617. There, influenced by the works of Adam Elsheimer, he developed a very detailed painting style, concentrating mainly on landscapes and religious and mythological subjects. By 1625 Poelenburgh was back in Utrecht, where he gained a large following and was an active member in the painters' guild. Included in his extremely successful career was a trip to England in 1637 at the invitation of Charles I.

Scenes from classical mythology were much favored by Poelenburgh, both during his stay in Italy and after his return to Utrecht. The demand for this kind of subject is suggested by the fact that shortly after his return to the Netherlands, Poelenburgh received from the State of Utrecht the large sum of 575 guilders for a painting of the Marriage of Peleus and Thetis, which was purchased as a gift for Princess Amalia van Solms.[2]

The scene depicted here has been described as simply a feast or gathering of the gods, but in fact it represents a more specific event: Psyche received into Olympus.

According to the popular story by the second-century Roman writer Lucius Apuleius,[3] the beautiful Psyche, after undergoing a number of trials imposed on her by Venus, was brought to Olympus, where her lover, Cupid, pleaded for her acceptance among the gods. In Poelenburgh's painting, the plump, dark-haired Psyche sits on a cloud next to Cupid, who points toward another dark-haired female. This woman, seated next to the helmeted figure of Mars, can be identified as Venus, mother of Cupid. Venus's commanding pose combined with the suppliant expression on the face of Psyche conveys the legendary unwillingness of Venus to accept her son's earthly lover. The goddess Ceres, identified by her attribute of fruits, kneels between the two women, suggesting, on the one hand, her loyalty to Venus and, on the other, her sympathy for Psyche. Mars, also shown in the precarious position between Venus and Psyche, takes the opportunity to catch a more than casual glimpse of the latter, reportedly the loveliest of mortal women.

The two main figures seated at the table behind Psyche appear to represent Juno and Jupiter. Like Ceres, Juno was sympathetic toward Psyche, but refused to assist her in order to remain faithful to Venus. It was Jupiter who finally made the decision to accept Psyche into the realm of the gods. His assertive pose clearly indicates his powerful position. On the table next to Jupiter's right hand stands a large gold pitcher, which most likely represents

23b Cornelis van Poelenburgh, *Psyche Brought by Mercury to Olympus*, oil on panel, 40 x 70.5 cm. Basel, Kunstmuseum

23c Raphael and School, *Psyche Received into the Realm of the Gods*, 1618–19, ceiling fresco, Rome, Villa Franesina (Photo: Alinari)

the container for the ambrosia that the king of the gods would eventually give to Psyche to taste, thus making her immortal.

None of the other gods gathered around the table can be identified with certainty, but the seated male figure with his arm pointed upward may represent Mercury, who was responsible for bringing Psyche up to the heavens. Barely visible in the clouds at the far right are two more figures (fig. 23a). Judging from their isolated position and the crown on the man's head, one may assume that this couple represents Pluto, god of the underworld, and his wife Proserpine, who played an important role in the long conflict between Venus and Psyche. The large, abandoned Roman structure, prominently situated in the idyllic landscape below, may represent the sumptuous palace in which Cupid and Psyche carried on their earthly love affair.

Poelenburgh painted at least one other scene from the story of Psyche and Cupid. That work (fig. 23b), in the Kunstmuseum, Basel, shows Mercury in the act of bringing Psyche to Olympus, and Cupid, again shown as a young child, takes a prominent position at the feet of Jupiter.

With its philosophical connotations of the union of the Soul and Desire, the story of Psyche was a popular theme in Renaissance art. Poelenburgh's interest in the antique legend may be linked to his reported interest in the works of Raphael.[4] The well-known ceiling frescoes by Raphael in the Villa Farnesina (1618/19), which treat the same subject, would certainly have been familiar to the Dutch artist. In Raphael's rendering of approximately the same scene (fig. 23c), Cupid appears twice: once at the left, represented as a child next to Psyche, and again at the right, as a youth pleading his cause before Jupiter.

It is quite possible that Poelenburgh's painting was made while he was in Rome. Its overall design bears strong connections to another picture that he painted there in 1624 (fig. 23d).[5] The dated work, which depicts a similar Olympian gathering above an Italian landscape, also shows the clouds covering the earth at the left and the figures receding into space toward the right. Like most of Poelenburgh's celestial scenes, the 1624 painting features a brilliant blue sky. By contrast, in this and the Basel painting the figures are surrounded by an abundance of dark, gray clouds. The gloomy atmosphere serves the artist well, for it suggests the personal differences and discord that accompanied Psyche's acceptance into Olympus.

23d Cornelis van Poelenburgh, *The Feast of the Gods,* 1624, oil on panel, 42.5 x 49.5 cm. London, private collection (Photo: Alan Jacobs Gallery)

1 This entry, partially obliterated, reads "POELENBURGH. Ecole hollandaise 17ᵉ/. . . festin des dieux. Bois. H. 0.32; L. 0. . . ."

2 First mentioned by C. Kramm, *De levens en werken der Hollandsche en Vlammsche kunstchilders* . . . 6 vols. (Amsterdam: Gebroeders Diederichs, 1857–64), 5:1295–96. This work is now in the Worlitz Schloss, no. 1013. I am grateful to Nicolette Sluyter for her comments on related works by Poelenburgh.

3 Lucius Apuleius *The Golden Ass* bks. 4–6.

4 This influence is noted by J. von Sandrart, *Teutsche Academie,* 2 vols. (Nuremburg: J. P. Miltenberger 1675–79), 2:305; and Houbraken, 1:128.

5 This painting was last recorded in 1973 with the Alan Jacobs Gallery, London. Two variants of the 1624 composition are known: one in the Herzog Anton Ulrich Museum, Brunswick (oil on panel, 39.6 x 53.4 cm; no. 786), the other in the Staatliche Gemäldegalerie, Kassel (oil on panel, 34.8 x 44.8 cm; no. GK 198). On the Kassel painting, the attribution to Poelenburgh is questioned.

Jan Porcellis

Ghent ca. 1584 – 1632 Zoeterwoude

24

Vessels on a Choppy Sea

Oil on canvas, 45.2 x 56.9 cm

Verso: Label with the number *211*; another with the numbers *383, 191*. Label inscribed *Charney / 13784-01.*

Provenance: Sale, Sotheby Parke Bernet, N.Y., 22–23 January 1976, no. 191 (as School of Jan Porcellis); private collection.

According to Houbraken, Porcellis was a student of the Haarlem marine painter Hendrick Vroom.[1] He was married in Rotterdam in 1605 and later traveled extensively, including a trip to England. After declaring bankruptcy in Rotterdam, he moved to Antwerp in 1615. Returning to Holland, he lived at different periods in Haarlem, Amsterdam, Voorburg (near The Hague) and finally in Zoeterwoude outside Leiden. His seascapes received continuous praise during the seventeenth century and were collected by well-known artists like Rembrandt and Rubens. His son Julius, also a marine painter, continued his father's late style.

This seascape appears to date from the early to mid-1620s, shortly before Porcellis turned to a monochromatic palette. The vessel in the foreground is a hooker, probably used for fishing. A little farther off to the left is a river barge with a spritsail. Unlike earlier marine painters who specialized in ship portraiture and depictions of specific naval events, Porcellis concentrated on the elements. Here a large part of the composition is given to the sky, whose variegated cloud formation adds significantly to the interest and drama of the scene. The water, treated in an extremely detailed manner, is characterized by strong chiaroscuro, which conveys the force and drama of the sea. Porcellis's interest in atmospheric effects can be seen in the background, where several vessels are almost completely obscured by the mist.

1 Houbraken, 1:213. For a discussion of Vroom's influence on Porcellis, see J. Walsh, Jr., "The Dutch Marine Painters Jan and Julius Porcellis," *The Burlington Magazine* 116, pts. 1 and 2 (November and December, 1974): 653–62, 734–44.

Hendrik Gerritsz. Pot

Haarlem (?) ca.1585 – 1657 Amsterdam

25

Scene in a Bordello

Oil on beveled panel, 35.5 x 41 cm

Signed lower right: HP

Verso: Label from 1956 Paris exhibition.

Provenance: Henri Leroux, Paris; sale, Palais Galliera, Paris, 23 March 1968, no. 76; H. Shickman Gallery, N.Y., 1968; private collection.

Exhibitions: *Le cabinet de l'amateur*, Musée de l'Orangerie, Paris, February–April 1956, no. 87 (*"Le galant soudard,"* lent by Henri Leroux); *Exhibition of Dutch and Flemish Paintings*, H. Shickman Gallery, N.Y., November 1968, no. 20.

Probably born in Haarlem, Pot is said to have been a pupil of Karel van Mander. In 1632 he visited London and painted portraits of the king and queen. He was an active member of the Haarlem Guild of St. Luke until about 1650, when he moved to Amsterdam. His oeuvre consists mainly of genre interiors and small-scale portraits.

In this brothel scene (*bordeltje*), Pot depicts the interaction of a procuress or madam, a prostitute, and a young man. The well-dressed man may represent a contemporary prodigal son, a subject that at the time enjoyed a vogue not only in Dutch painting, but also in Dutch literature and theater.[1] The clever juxtaposition of the aged procuress and the young prostitute forms an interesting *vanitas* image and at the same time implies the teamwork involved in the profession. While the young woman fondles her partner with one hand and receives money from him with the other, the old woman offers wine and tobacco, two vices that appear to have already had an effect on the red-eyed and seemingly intoxicated client.

The fashionable costumes and hair styles of the young couple date from the early 1630s. Judging from these styles and some of Pot's related paintings,[2] this work was probably executed shortly after, or possibly during, his 1632 trip to England. In fact, the proportions of the young man and woman, somewhat more elongated than the artist's usual figures, suggest the influence of Van Dyck, whose work Pot would have seen on his visit.

As in many of his interiors, Pot includes a framed painting on the back wall (fig. 25a). A combination of dunes and flatland, this landscape recalls the area around Haarlem where the artist spent most of his career. With its intense blue sky, rich golden-colored terrain, and dark black frame, the background picture is an assertive element and an important factor in the balance of the asymmetrical composition. Beneath the framed painting, a simple arrangement of a stool, chair, cushion, and diagonally placed sword echoes the basic design of the figures and table in the foreground.

25a Detail from *Scene in a Bordello*

25b Detail from *Scene in a Bordello*

Although Pot never specialized in still-life painting, the skillful placement and rendering of the objects against the back wall and on the table (fig. 25b) is proof of his ability in this area. The delicately painted arrangement on the table calls to mind the works of Pieter Claesz. (see p. 27) and Willem Claesz. Heda, two other Haarlem artists who by this time had popularized such compositions. Included in the still life and on the floor are oyster shells, which, like the egg shell in the foreground, may have further meaning in this particular context, for at this time both oysters and eggs were considered aphrodisiacs.[3] Pot, who incorporated oysters into almost all of his brothel scenes, was undoubtedly aware of their sexual connotations.

1 For a discussion of the prodigal son theme, see I. Bergström, "Rembrandt's Double-Portrait of Himself and Saskia at the Dresden Gallery," *Nederlands Kunsthistorisch Jaarboek* 17 (1966): 143–69.

2 See, for example, the work dated 1633 in the Museum Boymans-van Beuningen, Rotterdam, no. 1678.

3 For a discussion of the oyster and the egg as aphrodisiacs, see *Tot lering en vermaak*, pp. 202–5, 236–39, and 252 (egg).

Adam Pynacker

Pynacker 1621 – Amsterdam 1673

26

Barges along an Italian Shore

Oil on canvas: 52 x 61 cm

Signed lower left on barrel in the barge: APynacker

Provenance: A. Brod Gallery, London, 1957; private collection.

Literature: W. Stechow, *Italy through Dutch Eyes: Dutch Seventeenth Century Landscape Artists in Italy*, exh. cat. (Ann Arbor: University of Michigan Museum of Art, 1964), no. 52; *Wadsworth Atheneum Paintings: The Netherlands and the German-speaking Countries, Fifteenth-Nineteenth Centuries* (Hartford: Wadsworth Atheneum, 1978), p. 174.

26a Adam Pynacker, *River Barges by an Italian Shore*, oil on canvas, 43.5 x 58.5 cm. Hartford, Wadsworth Atheneum. The Ella Gallup Sumner and Mary Catlin Sumner Collection

Pynacker, born in a village near Delft from which he took his name, is reported to have spent three years in Italy. In 1649 he was living at Delft and in 1658 he is mentioned in Schiedam. He eventually settled in Amsterdam, where he painted large, decorative landscapes for wealthy Dutch burghers. In his early landscapes Pynacker was influenced by Jan Both and Jan Asselyn, but by around 1660 he had developed his own personal style.

Pynacker painted several coastal scenes like this one. An almost identical work in the Wadsworth Atheneum, Hartford (fig. 26a), suggests the popularity of this particular composition.[1] In comparison with the Hartford picture, this painting is slightly more vertical, which accounts for a larger sky and a steeper incline on the hill in the middle distance. So close are these two paintings, not only in their design, but also in their coloring and handling, one can assume they were executed about the same time, which according to Albert Blankert would have been late in the artist's career, around 1670.[2]

In both paintings, the artist creates a dream-like world by setting warm, yellow sunlight against soft, blue distances. From the foreground to the background, the scene is saturated with color, which gives the work its extremely luminous quality. The barges and the hills and mountains form a series of overlapping planes, which like the flats of a stage set play off each other in terms of both color and value to produce a vast, atmospheric space.

1 According to J. Nieuwstraten, another version, apparently a copy having the same measurements as the Hartford picture, was recently sold by Vermolen, The Hague. Closely related compositions by Pynacker include *A Boat on the Bank of a River*, Amsterdam, Rijksmuseum (cat. 1976, no. A2335) and *Landscape with a Barge*, lent by A. Brod, London, to the exhibition *Ideal and Classical Landscape*, Cardiff, National Museum of Wales, 2 February–3 April 1960 (no. 60, illus.).

2 A. Blankert, *Nederlandse 17e eeuwse italianiserende landschapschilders* (Soest-Holland: Davaco, 1978), p. 186, no. 1, p. 194, no. 2.

Pieter Jansz. Quast

Amsterdam 1605/6 – 1647 Amsterdam

27

Peasants in an Interior

Oil on beveled panel, 35.6 x 56.2 cm

Signed on barrel: PQast

Verso: Inscribed on the panel in 17th-century script *Hendrick*. Inscribed on paper border *Van Ostade*.

Provenance: Vose Galleries, Boston, 1958; private collection.

Quast began his career in Amsterdam, but in 1634 entered the painters' guild at The Hague. By 1644, however, he was back in Amsterdam, where he spent the rest of his life. His early works include painted illustrations of proverbs in the style of Adriaen van de Venne (see p. 113). Also an imitator of Adriaen Brouwer, Quast is best known for his scenes of soldiers, peasants, and merrymakers.

This work exhibits a much broader handling of paint than *An Elegant Company* (see following entry), which is dated 1639. The lively brushwork and vivid play of values make the painting seem more colorful than it actually is. Except for the intense red dress on the woman at the left, the color scheme is basically a close range of yellows, browns, and mauves.

In the tradition of Van de Venne, Quast uses his peasant scene to illustrate several themes, the most prominent being the Five Senses. The urinating child symbolizes Smell, while the apple being handed to him represents Taste. Another symbol of Taste is the man looking into the tankard. This tippler, whom the Dutch would appropriately call a *kannekijker* (literally "a tankard-watcher"), also symbolizes Sight.[1] The flute player next to the drinker refers to Hearing, and the pair of lovers in the background demonstrate quite graphically the sense of Touch (fig. 27a).

In Quast's painting, the Senses are specifically connected with vice. For example, the *kannekijker* refers to gluttony, and the shameless lovers imply sins of the flesh. The smoke that rises up behind the couple suggests the fleeting nature of profane love, a theme that Quast also treats in *An Elegant Company*. In this particular context, the flute being played by the rather coarse, bearded man has erotic connotations. Long associated with sensuousness and passion, the flute was used at this time as both a male sexual symbol and a metaphor for sexual activity itself.[2]

Another symbol of lust and sexuality is the goat, prominently placed in the right foreground. The goat may refer not only to the couple in the background, but also to the two bare-foot and earthy women shown taking care

of the small child. According to the Dutch artist and writer Karel van Mander, the goat, a symbol of unchastity, "signifies the whore, who destroys the
young people even as the goat gnaws off and ruins the young green
sprouts."[3]

The theme of the corruption of youth is also implied by the woman handing
the child an apple. This fruit, besides having connotations of the fall of man,
suggests the popular Dutch expression "one rotten apple spoils the whole
basket," here referring to the vulnerable situation of the child.[4] Given the
nature of his adult environment, one has every reason to be concerned about
the child's moral upbringing, for, to cite another well-known Dutch adage,
"the young ones chirrup as the old ones used to sing."

1 See P. J. J. van Thiel, "Marriage Symbolism in a Musical Party by Jan Miense Molenaer," *Simiolus* 2 (1967/68): 92–94, and S. Slive, *Frans Hals*, 3 vols., Kress Foundation Studies in the History of European Art, vol. 4 (London: Phaidon Press, 1970–74), 3: 36–37, no. 60.

2 See E. de Jongh, "Realisme en schijnrealisme in de Hollandse schilderkunst van de zeventiende eeuw," *Rembrandt en zijn tijd*, exh. cat. (Brussels: Europalia, 1971), p. 175, fig. 12, and A. McNeil Kettering, "Rembrandt's *Flute Player:* A Unique Treatment of Pastoral," *Simiolus* 9 (1977): pp. 19–44.

3 Van Mander, *Het schilder-boeck* . . . (Amsterdam: Jacob Pietersz. Wachter, 1618), bk. 2, p. 115.

4 "Eén rotte appel in de mand maakt al het gave fruit te schand." See *Tot lering en vermaak*, pp. 290–91.

Pieter Jansz. Quast

Amsterdam 1605/6 – 1647 Amsterdam

28

An Elegant Company

Oil on beveled panel, 46 x 64.4 cm

Signed and dated upper right on fireplace: PQ/1639

Verso: Printed entry from a Dutch catalogue.[1] Label inscribed (in Russian) *State Art Museum, Inv. No. 66.* Label with the number *29129/6b7.* Inscribed on the panel *22.25-29129/P. Quast* and *7409/И Э 442.*

Provenance: P. P. Semenov, Leningrad; sale, Internationales Kunst-und Auktions-Haus, Berlin, 8 October 1932, no. 313; dealer, John Streep, N.Y., 1963/64; private collection.

Literature: P. P. Semenov, *Studies in the History of Netherlandish Painting Based on Examples that are found in Public and Private Collections in St. Petersburg* (in Russian) (St. Petersburg, 1885), p. 306; P. P. Semenov, *Etudes sur les peintres des écoles hollandaise, flamande et néerlandaise qu'on trouve dans la collection Semenov et les autres collections publiques et privées de St. Pétersbourg* (St. Petersburg: Imprimerie "Hérold," 1906), p. 171; A. Bredius, "Pieter Jansz. Quast," *Oud-Holland* 20 (1902): 76; A. Wurzbach, *Niederländisches Künstler-Lexikon,* 3 vols. (Vienna-Leipzig: Verlag von Halm und Goldmann, 1906–11), 2:368 (as *Ein Menuettänzer*).

28a Emblem from Otto van Veen's *Amorum emblemata, figuris aeneis incisa . . . ,* Antwerp, 1608, p. 139 (Photo: The Newberry Library, Chicago)

This merry company was painted in 1639 while Quast was living in The Hague.[2] The artist accentuates the richly painted blue and cream-colored costumes of his principal figures by setting them against a thin, dark, monochromatic, brown background. For many of his details, Quast simply scratched directly into the wet paint, producing both dark tones against light, as in the lace of the costumes, and light tones against dark, as in the strings of the lute.

The extremely décolleté costumes of the women imply that the scene is a bordello. Considering this environment, the stylishly dressed young man in the center, who is shown escorting one of the women, could have been associated with the prodigal son, who squandered his property on such worldly pleasures.[3] The apparent life style of all the figures, including their extravagant attire, would have been considered reprehensible in Holland's Calvinistic society.

The man in the center points with his hat toward the smoky fire at the right side of the room. In this context, the fire no doubt has added meaning: moralizers of the day often compared love to fire, including, for example, Otto van Veen, whose Cupid placed next to a blazing fire (fig. 28a) illustrates the connection between love and the flame "that one cannot contain, nor

---

95

XLVI.

Amour de putain d'eſtoupe le feu
Reluit beaucoup & dure peu.

28b Emblem XLVI from Jacob Cats's *Spiegel van den ouden ende nieuwen tijdt . . .* , The Hague: Burchoorn, 1632, p. 138 (Photo: Koninklijke Bibliotheek, The Hague)

Amour de putain feu de paille.

extinguish." Fire was particularly used to symbolize fleeting or profane love, as expressed in an emblem (fig. 28b) from Jacob Cats's *Spiegel van den ouden ende nieuwen tijdt:*

A harlot's love, like fire of flax,
Shines brightly, but duration lacks.

That Quast was familiar with such proverbs is proven by his many illustrations of them.[4]

As in Quast's *Peasants in an Interior* (see preceding entry), the artist may have intended here a reference to the Five Senses, with Hearing represented by the music, Smell by the fire, Taste by the wine jug, Touch by the gloves worn by the women, and Sight by what appears to be a sheet of music held by the seated woman at the left. Although the setting is considerably more refined than in the earlier painting, the reason for including the Five Senses would have been the same: to warn against their being used as a means to sin.

---

1 PIETER QUAST (1606–1647) / Danspaar, man met luit, zittende dame en staand paar in een interieur. / Getekend met initialen en 1639.

2 On 15 January of that year, Quast bought a house in The Hague (A. Bredius, *Künstler-Inventare: Urkunden zur Geschichte der holländischen Kunst des XVI*[en]*, XVII*[en]* und XVIII*[en]* Jahrhunderts,* 8 vols. [The Hague: M. Nijhoff, 1915–22] 6 : 2097–121).

3 See also the painting by Pot, p. 85, including note 1.

4 For further discussion of this theme and related emblems, see *Tot lering en vermaak,* pp. 126–29.

Dirck Dircksz. Santvoort

Amsterdam 1610/11 – 1680 Amsterdam

29

A Dutch Family

Oil on beveled panel, 111.5 x 147 cm

Signed and dated lower left: D. D. Santvoort fe./164 . . .

Provenance: Sale, Amsterdam, C. F. Roos and C. F. Roos, Jr., 28 April 1875, no. 40; purchased by Roos; Albert Lestoque, Denver; John Nicholson Gallery, N.Y.; The Childs Gallery, Boston, 1967; private collection.

Exhibition: The Denver Art Museum, Denver, Colo., 4–28 November 1943 (lent by Albert Lestoque).

Santvoort was the son of the Amsterdam painter Dirck Pietersz. Bontepaert. Like his two brothers, who were also artists, he adopted the surname Santvoort. He probably trained with his father and in 1636 he became a master in the Amsterdam painters' guild. Specializing in portraiture, Santvoort painted many members of the upper class of Amsterdam, where he appears to have spent his entire life.

The last digit of the date on this painting is illegible. In 1875 the date was recorded as 1640, but in the catalogue for the 1943 Denver exhibition it was given as 1641. Either date is appropriate judging from the fashionable dress of the two children. The woman, on the other hand, wears a more traditional costume, in particular the millstone collar, which dates from the 1620s.

Santvoort shows little interest in the innovations in portrait painting that had been made by artists like Hals and Rembrandt. Instead, he works in a more traditional style, placing his figures in rather formal positions and painting them in a smooth, highly finished manner. Concentrating on exact likenesses, Santvoort gives the faces a characteristic porcelain-like quality, which is enhanced by the dark gray background. As in all his portraits, he works with a variety of rich fabrics, meticulously delineating their elaborate patterns and intricate lace trimmings. Particularly fascinating is his depiction of transparent materials, like the mother's cap, and his rendering of both sides of the same fabric, as seen in the young girl's upraised overdress.

It has been suggested that originally Santvoort's painting may have been larger and included a man, or that it was designed with a companion piece showing a man and perhaps additional children, as was common in Dutch family portraiture. Neither suggestion, however, seems to be correct. First of all, the back of the panel shows a beveled edge at both ends, indicating that the painting was not cut down. Secondly, considering the position of the woman in this painting, a pendant to it would have been designed to hang to the left, the traditional placement of the male portrait; but since the room depicted here is sealed off by a wall at the left, a second composition to be placed on that side would have no spatial connection with this one.

D. D. Santvoort fe,
164

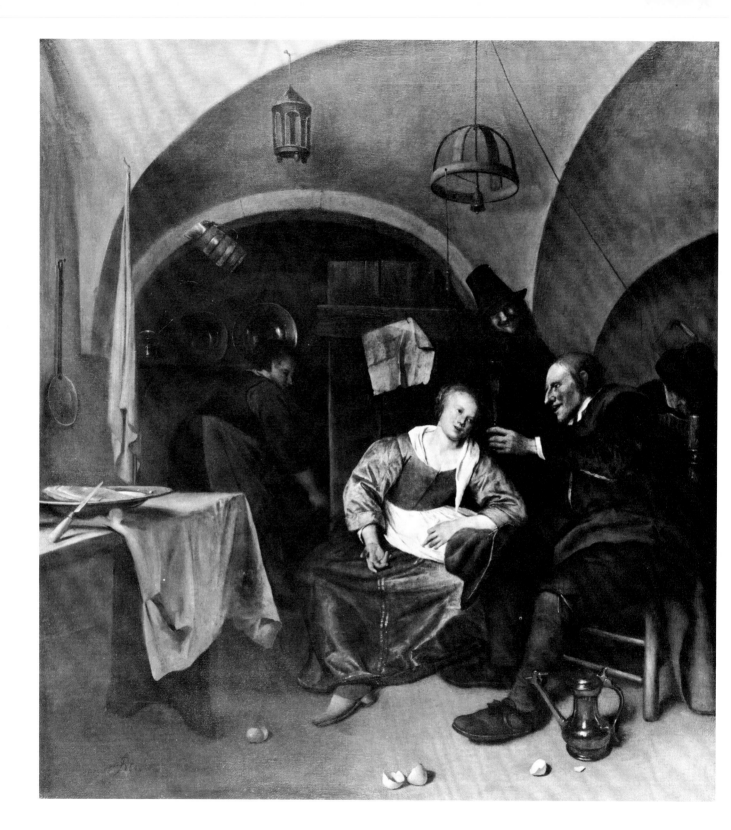

Jan Steen
Leiden 1625/6 – 1679 Leiden

30

Tavern Scene

Oil on canvas, 55 x 49.3 cm

Signed lower left: JSteen

Provenance: M. van Hoeken, The Hague, 1742; Theo. Hartsoeker, The Hague, 1742; R. Fort, Twyford; sale, Robinson and Fisher, London, 1 April 1897, no. 152; Thos. Agnew & Sons, Ltd., London, 1897; D. P. Sellar, 1897; Sir Charles Bagot, 1945; dealer, Eugene Slatter, London, 1947; sale, Palais des Beaux-Arts, Brussels, 15 March–16 June 1954, no. 436; private collection; sale, Christie's, London, 24 November 1967, no. 109; dealer, Adolphe Stein, Paris, 1967; H. Shickman Gallery, N.Y., 1968; private collection.

Exhibitions: *1947 Exhibition of Dutch and Flemish Masters*, Eugene Slatter Gallery, London, 14 May–28 June 1947, no. 23; *Exhibition of Dutch and Flemish Paintings*, H. Shickman Gallery, N.Y. November 1968, no. 13.

Literature: T. van Westrheene, *Jan Steen: Etude sur l'art en Hollande* (The Hague: M. Nijhoff, 1856), p. 155, no. 306; HdG, 1: no. 540; A. Graves, *Art Sales from Early in the Eighteenth Century to Early in the Twentieth Century*, 3 vols. (London: A. Graves, 1918–21), 3:178.

Steen was inscribed at the University of Leiden in 1646 at the age of twenty. For his artistic training he studied first with Nicolaus Knüpfer at Utrecht, then with Adriaen van Ostade at Haarlem, and finally with Jan van Goyen at The Hague. In 1648 he became a member of the Leiden Guild of St. Luke, and in the following year he was living at The Hague, where he married Jan van Goyen's daughter Margaretha. From 1654 to 1657 Steen resided at Delft; there he operated a brewery leased to him by his father. From Delft he moved to Warmond (near Leiden), where he stayed until 1661. He then settled in Haarlem and became an active member in the painters' guild. In 1670 Steen moved back to Leiden, where he inherited a house and in 1672 obtained permission to operate an inn. Extremely prolific, the artist specialized in genre scenes, but also painted portraits and religious and mythological subjects. His work reflects a strong sense of humor, an interest in the theater, and a tendency to moralize.

Judging from the thin application of pigment and overall cool tonality, this work appears to have been painted in the mid-1660s, a date that accords with the style of the young woman's costume.

The bell crown that hangs from the ceiling suggests that the setting is a public house, and the well-dressed young woman, who is the center of the scene, has apparently subjected herself to several of the vices connected with this type of environment. Her unlady-like pose, dazed expression, and loosened scarf imply that she is already a victim of the wine being offered her by

30a Jan Steen,*"The Broken Eggs,"*oil on canvas, 43.3 x 38.1 cm. London, National Gallery

her elderly male companion.[1] The theme of a well-dressed woman surrounded by the vices of an inn appears in several paintings by Steen, as, for example, *"The Broken Eggs"* (fig. 30a).[2]

An old man tempting a young woman was a popular subject with Steen. In this depiction he includes a likeness of himself in the man standing directly behind the ill-matched couple. Peering out from under his tall hat and wearing a broad grin, this jovial figure points out the folly of the situation. To the right of him can be seen a third man, who wears a hat and bends his head over as if asleep—probably the result of too much drink. Surrounded by cooking utensils, the old woman in the background seems to be responsible for the large plate of pancakes that lies on the table at the left. The pancake maker, another of Steen's favorite subjects, may have a special significance in this context since she is traditionally associated with lust and amorality.[3]

Broken egg shells scattered on the floor are common in Steen's interior scenes; but here, as in "The Broken Eggs," the prominently placed shells, like the pancakes, may add further meaning. As noted already (see p. 85), eggs were considered an aphrodisiac. In this particular scene they may also be a female sexual symbol,[4] just as the spouted flagon (*pijpkan*), or so-called Jan Steen-kan, on the floor next to the old man could be a phallic symbol.[5]

---

1 In several recent catalogue descriptions (1947, 1954, 1967), this man has been associated with Jan van Goyen, father-in-law of Steen; however, there is no evidence to support this identification. In fact, known portraits of Van Goyen show no resemblance to this figure; these include a drawing attributed to Jan de Bray (Gemeentemusea, Amsterdam) and a painting by Gerard ter Borch (Lichtenstein Collection, Vaduz). Both portraits are illustrated in H.-U. Beck, *Jan van Goyen 1596–1656: Ein Œuvreverzeichnis*, 2 vols. (Amsterdam: Van Gendt, 1972/73), 1:2 (De Bray) and 2:ii(Ter Borch).

2 For comments on this theme, see C. Brown, *Art in Seventeenth Century Holland*, exh. cat. (London: National Gallery, 1976), p. 87.

3 For a discussion of one of Steen's depictions of the pancake maker and the symbolism connected with this figure, see J. Markell's entry in *Dutch Life in the Golden Century*, exh. cat. (n.p., 1975), pp. 41–42.

4 For a discussion of some of the sexual symbols in "The Broken Eggs," see A. von Criegern, "Abfahrt von einem Wirtshaus: Ikonographische Studie zu einem Thema von Jan Steen," *Oud Holland* 86 (1971): 21. Broken eggs could represent the loss of virginity, a symbolism that becomes more explicit in the paintings of 18th-century French artist Jean-Baptiste Greuze; see E. Munhall, *Jean-Baptiste Greuze 1725–1805*, exh. cat. (Hartford: Wadsworth Atheneum, 1976), p. 40, no. 9.

5 As B. D. Kirschenbaum has noted, the still lifes of Steen often reiterate the eroticism of the pictures (*The Religious and Historical Paintings of Jan Steen* [New York: Allanheld & Schram, 1977], p. 72).

Abraham Storck

Amsterdam 1644 – after 1704 (?) Amsterdam (?)

31

Ships on a Calm Sea Near the Shore

Oil on beveled panel,[1] 27.8 x 32.1 cm

Signed lower left: A:Storck

Provenance: Private collection.

The son of an Amsterdam painter, Abraham Storck appears never to have moved from his native city, where he was a member of the Guild of St. Luke. His seascapes and Dutch harbor scenes suggest the influence of Ludolf Bakhuizen (see p. 13) and Willem van de Velde the Younger. Although Storck may never have left the Netherlands, he also painted numerous views of Mediterranean harbors in the style of Jan Beerstraaten and Jan Baptist Weenix.

This calm seascape,[2] which probably dates from about 1680,[3] exhibits a certain amount of restraint in comparison with the artist's later works, which are characterized by theatricality and excessive ornamentation. The intense blues of the sky and water serve to set off the warm tones of a variety of naval vessels. A States yacht (*statenjacht*) occupies the main position in the middle distance. Behind it, partially obscured by smoke, can be seen a barge with a rust-colored sail. To the left of the States yacht, a small boat filled with men sets off to meet two men-of-war, the crews of which mark their arrival by preparing to furl the sails. The shoreline with fishermen and rowboats silhouetted against the water serves as a *repoussoir* to the picturesque naval scene.

Storck focuses on details of human interest, like the flags, the rigging, the carving on the sterns of the ships, and the figures in the vessels and along the shore. He also capitalizes on numerous pictorial effects: the smoke of the gun salutes, the light and shadow on the sails, the rippled reflections on the water, and the blue and gray harmonies of the partially cloudy sky. This combination of realistic detail and colorful effects appears to have met with much favor, judging from the large number of works he produced in this style.

An eighteenth-century engraving by Jean Jacques le Veau (1729–1785) after an original drawing by Storck (fig. 31a) is virtually a mirror image of this painting.[4] Its present whereabouts unknown, the drawing appears to have been a preparatory study for either *Ships on a Calm Sea* or another closely related composition.[5] The only major difference between this painting and the drawing, as recorded by Le Veau, is the position of the man-of-war at the left (in the engraving, at the right). In the painting, the artist sets the large ship farther back, thereby giving more prominence to the smaller and more centrally placed States yacht.

Du Cabinet de M.ʳ Poullain

31a Jean Jacques Le Veau, after a drawing in bister by Abraham Storck, engraving, 123 x 158 mm. From B. F. Basan, *Collection de cent-vingt éstampes, gravées d'après les tableaux & dessins qui composoient le cabinet de M. Poullain . . . ,* Paris, 1781, no. 96 (Photo: The Metropolitan Museum of Art)

1 The panel is beveled at the top and on both sides (2 to 5 cm), but not at the bottom. Judging from the composition, the panel appears to have been cut down before the painting was made.

2 An extremely similar composition was recorded in 1949 in the collection of Conde de Torre-palma, Madrid (Photo: RKD).

3 See, for example, the pair of small seascapes dated 1683 in the Mauritshuis, The Hague (cat. 1977, nos. 173,174).

4 The drawing is the same size as Le Veau's engraving, 123 x 158 mm. The engraving appeared in B. F. Basan, *Collection de cent-vingt éstampes, gravées d'après les tableaux & dessins qui composoient le cabinet de M. Poullain* . . . (Paris, 1781), no. 96. In the same publication other engravings show reversals of original compositions.

5 See note 2 above.

Rombout van Troyen
Amsterdam 1605 – ca.1655/6 Amsterdam[1]

32

Solomon Sacrificing to the Idols

Oil on panel, 46.9 x 70 cm

Signed and dated lower right: 1647/RTroÿen fe./29 Augu

Provenance: Savoy Art & Auction Galleries, N.Y., 9 December 1960, no. 156; private collection.

Exhibition: Sterling and Francine Clark Art Institute, Williamstown, Mass., Summer 1977.

Van Troyen appears to have spent his entire life in Amsterdam. Although according to Houbraken the artist never went to Italy,[2] his oeuvre consists mainly of landscapes and scenes of underground grottos filled with antique ruins. A variety of religious and mythological subjects are incorporated into his paintings.

This signed and unusually fully dated painting is, both in terms of its size and number of figures, one of Van Troyen's most ambitious compositions. According to the Old Testament account (1 Kings 11), Solomon in his old age turned from the Lord his God to worship the idols of his 700 wives and 300 concubines.[3] Here, in one of Van Troyen's typical cavernous settings, the biblical king, dressed in a brilliant red robe and surrounded by several wives, genuflects before a sacrificial altar and an over-life-sized statue of Venus and Cupid. Two of the women next to Solomon wear pointed caps that appear Eastern in origin and may also have some ritual significance. Behind Solomon another woman prepares a goat for sacrifice, while a group of figures in the middle distance leads in a sacrificial bull.

To the right of Venus and Cupid are two statues of women bearing fruit.[4] Several more statues appear in the background; one can be identified as Hercules,[5] at the right of the entrance to the cave, and another as Jupiter, in the circular temple on the hill outside (fig. 32a). The circular temple with its colossal statue of Jupiter appears to have been inspired by earlier depictions of the famous monument at Olympia.[6] Here, the elevated temple may refer to Solomon's construction of hill-shrines for the gods of all his foreign wives.[7] Likewise, the massive, twisted column at the entrance to the cave may be a reference to the spiral columns long associated with Solomon's own temple.[8]

The painting shows Van Troyen's fascination with all types of illumination. The brilliant daylight outside the cave contrasts with a variety of artificial

32a Detail of *Solomon Sacrificing to the Idols*

lights inside, which include the unexplained spotlighting on the principal figures, the blazing sacrificial fire, the numerous candles and oil lamps, and the flame in the upraised heart of Venus. Dispersed throughout the cave, the many small, flickering sources of light join with the artist's lively drawing style to create the emotional atmosphere traditionally associated with this Old Testament account.

---

1 The date of Van Troyen's death is uncertain. Houbraken states that he died in 1650 (3:53); however, he apparently was still alive on 30 April 1653, when he was ordered to pay his landlord the rent for his house. When the marriage banns of his daughter Catherina were published on 6 January 1657, her parents were mentioned as deceased. The fact that an insolvent inventory was made up for Van Troyen on 29 October 1655 and that his belongings were sold at public auction between November 1655 and 17 February 1656 suggests that the artist may have died in the summer of 1655. Still, one should also consider a recently sold painting by Van Troyen signed and dated the following year: *The Tower of Babel,* 1656 (Christie's, N.Y., 15 June 1977, no. 34, illus.). For the new documentation on Van Troyen's life, I am grateful to S. A. C. Dudok van Heel, Gemeentelijke Archiefdienst van Amsterdam.

2 Houbraken, 3:53.

3 At least one other depiction of the Worship of Solomon by Van Troyen is recorded. This signed, smaller work (oil on panel, 29 x 29 cm) was sold by Van Pappelendam & Schouten to F. Muller (11–12 June 1889, no. 172).

4 The crescent-shaped form on the head of the statue at the left appears to be simply decoration rather than a pagan symbol or the attribute of Diana.

5 Van Troyen included a similar statue of Hercules in a drawing dated 1646 (Kunsthalle Bremen, no. 1249 a). In this drawing, which shows a priest killing a pagan prince, the statue is also used to represent a false god.

6 See, for example, the 16th-century engravings after Maerten van Heemskerck and Maerten de Vos, both illustrated in G. Brett, "The Seven Wonders of the World in the Renaissance," *The Art Quarterly* 12, no. 4 (1949): 339–58, figs. 1, 5.

7 "He built a hill-shrine for Kemosh, the loathsome god of Moab on the height to the east of Jerusalem, and for Molech, the loathsome god of the Ammonites. Thus he did for the gods to which all his foreign wives burnt offerings and made sacrifices" (1 Kings 11: 7–8).

8 One should note, however, that this type of twisted, stone structure appears in several of Van Troyen's grotto scenes, such as his *Christ Healing a Sick Woman,* also painted in 1647 (Sotheby's, London, 28 March 1979, no. 35, illus.).

Adriaen van de Venne

Delft 1589 – 1662 The Hague

33

"Kalis-Boud"

Oil on canvas, 39.5 x 26 cm

Inscribed lower right: Kalis-Boud

Provenance: Private collection, Austria; Alan Jacobs Gallery, London, 1973; private collection.

Exhibition: *Fine XVII Century Dutch and Flemish Old Masters*, Alan Jacobs Gallery, London, 1973 (as *The Travelling Copper-Tinker*).

Adriaen van de Venne trained with the goldsmith Simon Valck at Leiden and then with the grisaille painter Hieronymus van Diest at The Hague. From around 1614 to 1625 he was active in Middelburg, where he painted historical and mythological subjects as well as landscapes in the style of Pieter Bruegel. While in Middelburg, he also began making book illustrations for the Zeeland poet-moralists Jacob Cats and Johan de Brune. In 1625 Van de Venne moved to The Hague where he spent the rest of his life. An active member of the painters' guild there, he was also one of the founders of the painters' confraternity *Pictura*. While in The Hague, Van de Venne specialized in designs for prints and book illustrations as well as moralizing genre pictures, which like this painting were grisailles executed in varying tones of gray or brown.

"Kalis-Boud," identified by the gothic inscription on the banderole at the lower right, is the leader of the passengers on the Ship of Fools, a group symbolizing folly and vice in contemporary society. Van de Venne depicted the same character twice in his book *Belacchende werelt* ("ridiculous world"), a humorous, moralistic work published in 1635.[1] In the author's preparatory drawing for the title page (fig. 33a), the ragged and unkempt Kalis-Boud takes a pose similar to that found in the painting.[2] An engraved illustration from the same book, also designed by Van de Venne (fig. 33b),[3] shows this disreputable character leading his band of shabby folk toward the *"Boot van Reyn-uyt,"* the Dutch Ship of Fools. In both book illustrations, Kalis-Boud carries as a standard two clay pipes mounted on a pole; a similar pair hangs from his waist in the painting. In both the painting and engraving, he is followed by a drummer and a flag bearer. The flag in the engraving shows a pitcher upside down like the one that hangs from his waist. The pitcher and clay pipes are both symbols of vice, referring to drinking and smoking.[4]

Van de Venne, who was extremely fond of homonyms, often gave his moralizing images titles that had more than one meaning.[5] *Kalis* is a word the gypsies used to describe themselves. In the vernacular, it meant "vagabond," "hobo," or "beggar." *Kalis* was also linked with the Dutch adjective

kaal ("bald," "bare") and took on the meaning of "shabby" or "beggarly." With these connotations, it is easy to see how the term *kalis* came to be associated with the Ship of Fools, which itself was referred to as the *Kalis schuit*.[6] *Boud* is synonymous with the English word *bold*, having unfavorable connotations like "arrogant" and "impudent." In Old German, the word *boud* was also used in various forms: in proper names, like Theobald or Humbold, and nouns that in general have negative connotations, like *dronkenbout* ("drunkard") or *schuifelbout* ("shuffler").[7] In fact, in Van de Venne's *Belacchende werelt*, Kalis-Boud is given another name, "Oude Roem-boud,"[8] which, besides being a play on the Christian name Rombout, also means "old braggart."[9] Therefore, the title *Kalis-Boud* can be translated as "shabby-man" or "pauper," as "bold or impudent tramp," or as "shabby and arrogant."[10]

Kalis-Boud's many associations with vice make him an undesirable figure in an ideal society. The straw that covers him and the useless pitcher that hangs at his side both hint at his worthlessness. Yet among his own class, Kalis-Boud holds an important position, which Van de Venne acknowledges by depicting him as a leader. Advancing toward the viewer with a confident stride, he is seen from below—a perspective which not only increases his own stature, but at the same time dwarfs his followers. Adding to the "shabby-official" image are the walking stick, the helmet which consists of a large leaf, and the pair of makeshift epaulets—a bowl and basket. This humorous combination of contrasting elements, like the punning title, is indicative of Van de Venne's entertaining approach to moralizing.

33a Adriaen van de Venne, detail from preparatory drawing dated 1634 for title page of his *Belacchende werelt* . . . , pen and brown wash on paper, 177 x 136 mm. Coburg, Kunstsammlungen Veste Coburg

33b *"De Boot van Reyn-uyt,"* after Adriaen van de Venne, from *Belacchende werelt . . . ,* Middelburg: A. van de Venne, 1635, p. 158 (Photo: Koninklijke Bibliotheek, The Hague)

1 A. van de Venne, *Tafereel van de belacchende werelt* . . . (The Hague: A. van de Venne, 1635), pp. iii, 158.

2 The painting appears to have been done about the same time as the drawing, in 1634.

3 According to D. Franken, all eleven engravings in the book were designed by Van de Venne himself (*Adriaen van de Venne* [Amsterdam: C. M. van Gogh, 1878], pp. 98–99).

4 See p. 73.

5 See, for example, the multiple meanings of one of Van de Venne's favorite titles, *Al-arm,* discussed in *Tot lering en vermaak,* pp. 254–57.

6 M. de Vries et al., eds., *Woordenboek der Nederlandsche taal* (The Hague: M. Nijhoff, 1882–), vol. 7, pt. 1, cols. 965–70 (hereafter cited as WNT). C. Tuinman, *Zedenzangen, . . .* (Leiden: J. A. Langerak, 1720), pp.102–3, is cited as a source for the expression *Kalis schuit.*

7 WNT, vol. 3, pt. 1, cols. 748–51.

8 In *Belacchende werelt,* the name is spelled both *Roem-bout* (p. xv) and *Roem-boud* (p. 157).

9 The equivalent of this meaning of *bout* in English is the suffix "art" or "ard," as in "braggart" or "dullard."

10 For their assistance on the various meanings of *Kalis-Boud,* I am grateful to K. van der Horst and H. Nalis.

Hendrik Cornelisz. van Vliet

Delft 1611/12 – 1675 Delft

34

Oude Kerk, Delft

Oil on beveled panel, 47.3 x 44.3 cm

Provenance: Duits Ltd., Amsterdam, 1924; dealer Gebr. Douwes, Amsterdam, 1924/25; bought by Dr. Schaeffer, Berlin, 1925; sold by Schaeffer Galleries, Inc., N.Y., 1948; private collection.

34a Hendrik Cornelisz. van Vliet, *Church Interior* (Oude Kerk in Delft), 1671, oil on panel, 52 x 42.5 cm. Vienna, Gemäldegalerie der Akademie der bildenden Künste

Van Vliet, who was trained by his uncle Willem van Vliet and Michiel van Miereveld, began his career as a portrait painter. In 1632 he entered the Delft painters' guild, and it was not until about twenty years later that he began painting architectural scenes. Greatly influenced by the Delft architectural painter Gerard Houckgeest, Van Vliet specialized in interior views of the two main churches in his home town.

This particular view inside the Old Church was repeated throughout Van Vliet's career. It should be compared, for example, to his painting dated 1671 in Vienna (fig. 34a).[1] Like the Vienna picture, this work was also painted late in the artist's career, when his palette included a wide range of hues—from the cool, rose violet in the vaulting of the transept to the warm yellow in the patches of strong sunlight.[2]

To convey the vastness and the three-dimensionality of the church interior, Van Vliet introduces all kinds of illusionistic devices. First of all, by taking an oblique viewpoint, he manages to juxtapose forms both near and far; the contrasts of color and scale that result emphasize the great distances in between. Secondly, he places two large pillars in the immediate foreground that force the viewer to look in several different directions and thereby appreciate the multiplicity of the large interior space. Thirdly, he makes the farthermost part of the church the lightest, which serves to draw the viewer into the depth; and finally, he inserts figures and animals throughout, which not only call attention to the many different areas, but, because of their diminuative size, also give an exaggerated sense of scale.

Van Vliet took his view from the south aisle facing the north transept. If one sees the interior from this same position, it becomes obvious that the painter interpreted rather freely certain architectural elements as well as the perspective. In general, the architectural changes help to stress the verticality of the space.[3] Van Vliet also took liberties with the placement of objects. For example, the pulpit, which differs in style from the original, which can be seen in the Vienna painting (fig. 34a), appears here on the left side of the nave instead of on the right.[4] In addition, the sculptural relief prominently displayed on the foremost pillar appears out of its proper setting. Taken from its original location in the choir area, where it can still be seen today, this Baroque monument (fig. 34b), dated 1644, honors the important town official Johan van Lodensteyn (1557–1626) and his wife, Maria van Bleyswyck.[5]

One of Van Vliet's favorite monuments, the Van Lodensteyn relief appears in many of his views inside the Old Church.[6] Its combination of putti and a skull is a traditional symbol of the transience of life.[7] Together with the surrounding memorial tablets and the grave digging at the lower right, the

PIÆ·MEMORIÆ
PATRIS·CHARISSIMI
IOHANNISALODENSTEŸN
CONSVLISDELPHENSIS
ET·MATRISDVLCISSIMÆ
MARIÆ·ABLEYSWYCK
FILIVS·VNICVS·EDVARDVS
A·LODENSTEŸN·EIVSDEM
VRBIS·CONSVL·HOC
MONVMENTVM
PONI·CVRAVIT
M·DI·XLIV·

34b Monument of Johan van Lodensteyn and
Maria van Bleyswyck, 1644. Oude Kerk, Delft
(Photo: courtesy Gemeentearchief Delft)

centrally placed monument helps to make the church interior an appropriate reminder of the brevity of man's existence.[8] As a memorial to a deceased leader, the Van Lodensteyn monument also hints at the transitoriness of glory, another well-known theme in Baroque art.

1 Similar views by Van Vliet are found in the Szépmüvészeti Muzeum, Budapest (cat. 1968, no. 405, ascribed to Jacob van der Ulft), and the Alte Pinakothek, Munich (cat. 1958, no. W.A.F. 1161). H. Jantzen compared the Budapest and the Munich picture, dating the latter at the beginning of the 1660s (*Das niederländische Architekturbild* [Leipzig: Klinkhardt und Biermann, 1910], p. 104).

2 For a color description of the Vienna painting, see R. Eigenberger, *Die Gemäldegalerie der Akademie der bildenden Künste in Wien*, 2 vols. (Vienna-Leipzig: Manz Verlag, 1927), 1:439–40.

3 For example, the bases of the foreground pillars are increased in height and the nearest opening of the east arcade in the north transept, which is actually a wide opening with a round arch (see fig. 34a), has been divided into two narrow units with pointed arches.

4 Van Vliet included the same pulpit, also on the left side of the nave, in the Budapest and Munich paintings (see n. 1 above).

5 The Van Lodensteyn monument hangs on the south side of the middlemost pillar of the choir. See E. A. van Beresteyn, *Grafmonumenten en grafzerken in de Oude Kerk te Delft* (Assen: Van Gorcum & Co., 1938), p. 20, no. 6. An 18th-century engraving showing the coat of arms (which is now missing) at the top appears in P. Timareten, *Verzameling van gedenkstukken in Nederland* . . . , 3 vols. (The Hague, 1775–81), 1:130, no. 5.

6 It appears in paintings by Van Vliet in the Rijksmuseum, Amsterdam (dated 1654); the Mauritshuis, The Hague; the Staatliche Gemäldegalerie Kassel; the Manchester City Art Gallery; and the Philadelphia Museum of Art (dated 1659).

7 For a discussion of this motif, see H. W. Janson, "The Putto with the Death's Head," *The Art Bulletin* 19 (1937):423–49.

8 For some of the religious meanings incorporated into depictions of church interiors, see *Die Sprache der Bilder*, exh. cat. (Braunschweig, 1978), pp. 92–95, 170–73.

Jan Vonck

Torun (Poland) 1631 – 1663/4 Amsterdam [1]

35, 36

Still Life with a Kingfisher

Oil on beveled panel, 36 x 32 cm

Still Life with a Male Bullfinch

Oil on beveled panel, 36 x 32 cm

Provenance for both works: Dealer, A. Castagno, Boston; private collection.

Jan Vonck appears to have been a student of his father, Elias (died 1652),[2] one of the founders of the Dutch tradition of the game still life. Like his father, he generally painted simple, monochromatic compositions, as opposed to the ornate and more colorful works of the Flemish tradition. The younger Vonck's favorite subjects were birds and fish.

Considering their identical size and the complementary quality of their over-all color and design, one can assume that these two paintings were intended as pendants.[3] As with many subjects in Dutch art, still lifes were often painted as pairs, but unfortunately over the years vast numbers of them have been separated. By contrast, these two works, the provenance of which is unknown, appear to have always been together.

In both works the subject is simple: a few birds on a stone table. The painting at the left features a kingfisher (*Alcedo atthis*), surrounded by several chaffinches (*Fringilla coelebs*). A beautifully executed male bullfinch (*Pyrrhula pyrrhula*) occupies the main position in the work at the right. With one leg suspended from above by a string, he is arranged so that both wings fall away from his body forming two graceful, fan-like designs. Next to the bullfinch lies a female Great Tit (*Parus major*), and behind that what appears to be another chaffinch.[4]

Vonck achieves a certain intimacy by setting the birds against the dark, warm background and illuminating them with a soft, focused light. To reveal their colorful undersides, he places all of the birds in unnatural positions, making the keynote of color in both paintings the intense red of the main bird.

Using thin glazes and a minimal amount of impasto, Vonck achieves an extremely transparent quality throughout. His brushwork, like the subjects it describes, is light and delicate and, although very summary, gives an impression of great detail.[5] Particularly convincing is the tactile quality of the fine plumage, especially that of the bullfinch, whose shiny, stiff wing and tail feathers contrast with his soft, fluffy down (fig. 36a).

Game pieces like these were a favorite of the hunter. As Scott Sullivan suggests, the same works were probably also collected by non-hunters, who for reasons of prestige wished to be associated with the sports of the nobility.[6] Like the many paintings it inspired, the aristocratic sport of fowling enjoyed a great vogue in the northern Netherlands during the second half of the century.[7]

36a Detail from *Still Life with a Male Bullfinch*

1 The year and place of the artist's birth is taken from an Amsterdam marriage announcement of 6 December 1653 for a painter named Johannes Vonck who appears to be the artist under consideration. One can assume that Jan Vonck was still alive in 1663, the year of his latest, known dated works (see, for example, the signed and dated still life exhibited by W. A. Martin and Brian Sewell, London, 24 November–2 January 1971, no. 18, illus.). The artist was dead, however, by 4 October of the following year, when his widow announced her second marriage.

2 Elias died in Amsterdam. He is first mentioned there on 22 May 1639, the baptismal date of one of his daughters. There are no records of his birth or marriage in Amsterdam; instead, it appears he went there in the 1630s, probably from Torun, Poland, where his son Jan was born in 1631. For the new archival information on Elias and Jan Vonck, I am grateful to S. A. C. Dudok van Heel, Gemeentelijke Archiefdienst van Amsterdam.

3 Vonck's father painted a pair of still lifes that includes dead birds. These paintings, one of which is signed and dated 1650, are reproduced in P. Gammelbo, *Dutch Still-Life Painting from the 16th to the 18th Centuries in Danish Collections* (Copenhagen: Munksgaard, 1960), pp. 28–29, nos. 24, 25. Closer in composition to the two paintings by Jan Vonck is the pair of dead bird still lifes by Cornelis Lelienbergh, both signed and dated 1655, in the Rijksmuseum, Amsterdam (cat. 1976, nos. A1454, A1455).

4 The identifications of the various species were made by Dr. G. F. Mees of the Rijksmuseum van Natuurlijke Historie, Leiden.

5 The same sketchy quality appears in one of Vonck's bird still lifes signed and dated 1659 (Rotterdam, Museum Boymans-van Beuningen), as well as two other signed, but undated, works (Sotheby's, London, 30 April 1958, no. 161 and Christie's, London, 2 July 1976, no. 39).

6 S. A. Sullivan, "The Dutch Game Piece," (Ph.D. diss., Case Western Reserve University, 1978), pp. 123–24.

7 See, for example, the painting by Abraham Hondius, p. 39.

Jan de Vos IV

Leiden 1618 – 1664 Leiden

37

Panoramic Landscape

Oil on beveled panel, 71.4 x 140.5 cm

Signed and dated lower left: VOS. 1641

Verso: Agnew label, no. 7061. Label inscribed *Anthonie Jansz. van de Croos*. Label from the Museum of Fine Arts, Boston, no. TL 7518 (conservation work, Nov. 1950–Jan. 1951). Circular orange sticker with number *956*.

Provenance: Lady Millicent Hawes, Stafford House Collection (as by Jan de Vos); Thos. Agnew & Sons, Ltd., London, 1920 (attribution changed to Anthonie Jansz. van der Croos); purchased from Agnew in 1930 by Mrs. R. T. Crane, Ipswich, Mass.; sale, Estate of Florence H. Crane, Ipswich (Parke-Bernet, N.Y.), 1 July 1950, no. 956 (as by van der Croos, "with initials V.C., and dated 1649"); private collection.

This painting is closely related to another large, panoramic landscape with the same inscription: VOS 1641 (fig. 37a).[1] The other work, entitled *View of Noordwijck*, depicts an area near the dunes not far from Leiden. In this painting, however, the water mill, the large expanse of hilly terrain, and the architectural style of the castle in the right distance all suggest a setting in or near Germany, rather than a scene around the artist's native town. That the author of this work probably traveled to Germany is suggested by another painting, *View of Cologne* (fig. 37b), signed and dated the same year as this landscape.[2] According to Hofstede de Groot, the *View of Cologne* and the *View of Noordwijck* are by the same hand.[3]

Since the De Vos family included at least four painters, all having the same first name Jan, it has been a problem assigning the works that bear this name. As Bredius points out, the name Jan de Vos appears in the Leiden painters' guild almost continuously between the years 1644 and 1682.[4] Bredius attempted to sort out the relationship between these painters; however, more recently P. J. M. de Baar of the Leiden City Archives has uncovered new information that helps to establish the authorship of this and other related works.[5]

Jan de Vos II (1615–1691), like his father, Jan I (ca.1593–ca.1671), was married and had a family by 1641. Both were referred to as *kladschilders* or "house painters," and therefore would probably not have left the place of their business during the summer months, when this landscape appears to have been painted. Jan III (1636–1693), who was a half-brother of Jan II,[6] was only five years old in 1641 and therefore could not be the artist. Instead, this picture appears to be by Jan IV, Jan I's first cousin, who in 1641 was

37a Jan de Vos, *View of Noordwijck*, 1641, oil on panel, 44.8 x 86 cm. Present whereabouts unknown (Photo: courtesy Kunstmuseum Düsseldorf)

37b Jan de Vos, *View of Cologne*, 1641, oil on panel, 32 x 65 cm. Stockholm, National Museum

twenty-three years of age and unmarried.[7] An orphan at the age of six, Jan IV had as one of his guardians from 1636 to 1639 the Leiden landscape painter Pieter de Neyn. The influence of De Neyn, who died in 1639, is evident in this work, particularly in the figures and the large tree at the left, which is characterized by twisted branches and spotted foliage.

Here De Vos continues the Flemish tradition of three distinct bands of color: warm brown in the foreground, green in the middle distance, and blue gray in the background. The hill at the left, with its tree silhouetted against the sky and framing the sprawling terrain, is a pictorial device also seen in earlier landscapes. A similar *repoussoir* form appears in the *View of Noordwijck* (fig. 37a), as well as in the only drawing assigned to De Vos.[8] More modern elements in De Vos's painting are the vast sky, the low horizon, and the gradual progression into space, all of which show the influence of De Neyn and innovators like Molyn and Van Goyen.

The numerous figures in De Vos's painting help to give a sense of scale to the vast landscape and to lead the viewer into the distance. One of them, in the middle foreground, has a fox on a leash (fig. 37c); the animal may be a play on the artist's surname. A fox also occurs in a view of Leiden signed *Vos* and dated 1662.[9]

37c Detail of *Panoramic Landscape*

---

1 *View of Noordwijck* was on loan from the art dealer Bammann to the Kunstmuseum Düsseldorf from 1935 to 1948, when it went to the art dealer Ursula Stuckert, Wangen über Radolfzell, Germany.

2 Another view of Cologne which appears to be by the same hand is in the Szépmüvészeti Muzeum, Budapest (cat. 1968, no. 563).

3 C. Hofstede de Groot, "Jan de Vos och hans Utsikt av Köln," *Nationalmusei Årsbok* 11 (1929): 76–80.

4 A. Bredius, *Künstler-Inventare: Urkunden zur Geschichte der holländischen Kunst des XVI[ten], XVII[ten] und XVIII[ten] Jahrhunderts*, 8 vols. (The Hague: M. Nijhoff, 1915–22), 6: 2097–121.

5 Mr. de Baar plans to publish his recently discovered documents on the De Vos family.

6 In the documents, the two half-brothers are frequently referred to as *de ouder* and *de jonger*.

7 Jan IV married on 23 August 1646; see Bredius, *Künstler-Inventare*, 6: 2115.

8 *View of a River Landscape*, red chalk, 151 x 358 mm, The Royal Museum of Fine Arts, Copenhagen, no. Tu 66-la.

9 This painting was formerly on loan to the Lakenhal, Leiden (Photo: RKD).

Jan Wijnants

Haarlem ca.1630 – 1684 Amsterdam

38

Landscape with a Medieval Church

Oil on panel, 38 x 48 cm

Signed lower right: JWyna(nts)

Verso: Stenciled on panel *BC*. A letter written in French, pasted to the panel. Export stamp written in German.

Provenance: French collection (?);[1] A. L. Spitzer, Vienna; sale, C. J. Wawra, Vienna, 24 January 1906, no. 170; L. Lilienfeld, Vienna; sale, Sotheby, Parke-Bernet, N.Y., 17–18 May 1972, no. 53; private collection.

Literature: G. Glück, *Niederländische Gemälde aus der Sammlung des Herrn Dr. Leon Lilienfeld in Wien* (Vienna: Verlag der Gesellschaft für Verielfältigende Kunst, 1917), pp. 46–47, no. 82; HdG, 8: no. 488.

Wijnants spent his early career in Haarlem and from 1660 until his death is recorded in Amsterdam, where in 1672 he was described as a "painter and inn keeper." His oeuvre, which includes a large number of paintings, consists almost entirely of landscapes, most of which are scenes in the dunes around Haarlem.

This painting, characterized by its pleasant balance of warm and cool tones and crisp, delicate treatment throughout, can be compared with several of Wijnants's works dated 1659,[2] which according to current thought would be relatively early in the artist's career.[3] As in many of his paintings, Wijnants builds his composition around a road that winds into the distance, here skirted on one side by a motley, picturesque old fence and on the other by a small waterway. The artist's rather bold placement of the two large oak trees in the exact center of the composition goes almost unnoticed because of the great variety in the surrounding terrain.

The two isolated wood structures that appear in the middle distance (fig. 38a) were a common sight along the canal-enclosed fields of the Netherlands. They are gates, which in this case prevent livestock from crossing the bridges that span the canal. A frontal view of the same type of structure, though somewhat more decorative, appears in Claes Molenaer's *Landscape with a Bleaching Field* (p. 63).

A true landscape specialist working in the tradition of Jacob van Ruisdael, Wijnants gives full attention to the shapes and textures of the land itself. The few buildings, and even the sky, are clearly secondary. Likewise, the figures and animals are incorporated mainly to give a sense of scale and to mark out the many different areas. The figures, like those in most of Wijnants's land-

38a Detail from *Landscape with a Medieval Church*

scapes, appear to be by another hand, in this case Adriaen van de Velde, who according to Houbraken was a pupil of Wijnants.[4]

1 A French collector or dealer, or both, is suggested by an old, probably early 19th-century letter pasted to the back of the painting. The letter, greatly obliterated, includes the following: "puisque vous . . . Philipps Wou(werman) . . . il faut ou un Ruisd(ael) . . . ou un Winants: je (v)ous envoie un petit tableau de ce dernier maitre."

2 See, for example, his landscape in the Kunsthalle, Hamburg (oil on panel, 25 x 33 cm; cat. 1966, no. 225; HdG, 8: no. 355) and *The Withered Oak* (coll. Dr. Terman, Stockholm, oil on canvas, 58 x 49 cm; HdG, 8: no. 352 [Photo: Witt]). *The Withered Oak* includes in the foreground a similar peasant woman and child also shown walking along a road toward the viewer.

3 Stechow considered 1654 the earliest reliable date on a Wijnants painting. For his discussion on the subject, see "View of the Heerengracht, Amsterdam," *Cleveland Museum of Art Bulletin* 52 (1965):166.

4 Houbraken, 3:90.

Philips Wouwerman
Haarlem 1619 – 1668 Haarlem

39

Mounted Farrier Leading a White Horse

Oil on slightly irregular, circular beveled panel, 24.6 x 24.2 cm

Signed lower right: PH W

Provenance: Private collection, France; private collection.

39a Philips Wouwerman, *The Rest*, 1646, oil on panel, 32.3 x 36.2 cm. Leipzig, Museum der bildenden Künste

The eldest son of a painter, Wouwerman is said to have been a pupil of Frans Hals; however, the greatest influence on his work seems to have come from the genre painter Pieter van Laer, who returned from Italy to Haarlem in 1638. Wouwerman appears to have spent most of his life in Haarlem, where he was a member of the Guild of St. Luke. Extremely prolific, he painted mainly landscapes and small-scale genre scenes, most of which include horses. Wouwerman's paintings enjoyed a great vogue not only in his own time, but also during the eighteenth century, when a great number of them were engraved.

Wouwerman, considered Holland's greatest horse painter, here attempts an unusual view of a rearing horse. His successful treatment of difficult passages like the foreshortened torso and the tense rear leg muscles is proof of his knowledge of equine anatomy. Concentrating more on value than color, he creates a compositional tour de force by placing the dark-colored horse against a light background and the white horse against a dark background. The physical and visual tension between the two animals is further heightened by the barking dog that appears directly between them.

Circular paintings are extremely rare in Wouwerman's oeuvre.[1] In Hofstede de Groot's catalogue raisonné on the artist, which includes more than two thousand paintings, only two are mentioned.[2] Judging from the few dated works by Wouwerman, this painting appears to have been executed relatively early in his career, around the mid-1640s. It should be compared with the artist's 1646 painting *The Rest* (fig. 39a), which also features a light- and a dark-colored animal set against backgrounds of contrasting value.

1 Another circular painting, clearly based on this composition, was recorded on the European market about a decade ago.

2 HdG, 2: nos. 985b and 1009b. No. 985b, "A Sea-Shore.—A boy with two horses," may possibly be identical with this painting (circular panel, 9 inches across [23.4 cm]; sale, M. Van den Berg, Rotterdam, 19 June 1786, no. 24 [154 florins, Beekman]). The other tondo, entitled *Faggot Gatherers* (circular panel, 19 cm), has since been exhibited by M. Knoedler & Co., N.Y., 5–24 February 1945, no. 20.

Dominicus van Wynen, called Ascanius

Amsterdam 1661 – (?)

40

Divine Cosmos

Oil on canvas, 48 x 31 cm

Inscribed on book at lower left: EVANGEL / DUM

Provenance: Dealer, Julius H. Weitzner, London; Anthony M. Clark, Minneapolis and N.Y., 1977; private collection.

40a Detail of *Divine Cosmos*

In 1674 Van Wynen studied at The Hague with the history painter Willem Doudyns. He eventually traveled to Rome, where between 1680 and 1690 he was an active member of the organization of Netherlandish artists called the *Schildersbent*. Like all artists in this society, he took a nickname: Ascanius. His works, which are rather rare, include mythological, allegorical, and religious subjects.

The attribution of this painting is based on its similarity to several works by Van Wynen that also incorporate cosmic elements.[1] Like most of his surviving paintings, it appears to have been executed in Italy. The highly illusionistic composition and brilliant palette, dominated by blues and yellows, show the influence of late seventeenth-century Italian religious painting.

In the lower part of the painting the physical universe is shown as a large blue sphere. According to the Ptolemaic system, the earth is at the center; the sun appears off to the left. The cornucopia held by two angels below appears to symbolize the abundance of nature. Divinity is represented at the top of the painting by the golden sphere surrounded by tongues of fire. The other four spheres may represent the four elements that make up the material universe. Starting at the top right and going counterclockwise, there is the dark sphere of Earth, the transparent blue sphere of water, the sphere of air that surrounds the earth, and finally the sphere of ethereal fire that was thought to lie beyond Earth's atmosphere.[2]

The sphere of divinity at the top includes references to both the First and Third Persons of the Holy Trinity. The Hebrew characters at the center of the sphere—*he, aleph* and *lamedh*—allude to God the Father,[3] while the seven tongues of fire represent the Holy Spirit. Christ, the remaining Person of the Trinity, stands below to the right (fig. 40a), facing the sphere and linked to it by several intersecting rays. The letters *aleph* and *lamedh* are repeated where two of the rays touch his hands, confirming his identification with God.

Christ, who wears a crown of glory, is shown in the act of returning to the divine sphere in what might be called a cosmic ascension. At his left hand, angels bear instruments of the passion,[4] and on his right, symbols of sovereignity and immortality.[5] The ray of light that joins Christ to the Godhead is echoed on the left side of the composition by a beam of light that passes from the divine sphere at the top to the sun in the physical universe below. The sun in turn illuminates the earth and the rest of the solar system. This transferal of light from God to the world symbolizes, in an almost scientific manner, Christ's role as savior of the world or redeemer of mankind.

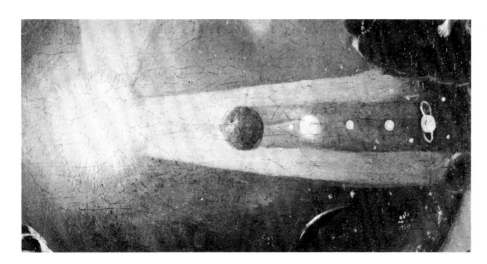

The gospel of St. John with its many references to Christ as "the light of the world" is the most obvious source for imagery of this kind.[6] The book held by the angel at the lower left is probably this gospel.[7] The angel with the book points to the larger angel next to him, who provides the key to the painting's meaning. This angel points with one hand toward the divine sphere and with the other toward the sun in the physical universe.

Van Wynen's religious imagery is enhanced by a rather detailed and scientific representation of the universe (fig. 40b).[8] It is not surprising to find that the artist used for his religious painting the Ptolemaic system, for at the time the work was painted, the heliocentric system of Copernicus, though supported throughout the century by the findings of Galileo and others, was still not accepted by the Roman Catholic Church. In spite of its geocentric arrangement, Van Wynen's depiction of the universe does include several modern observations. For example, Saturn, which appears at the far right, is shown with a ring. When first observed by Galileo in 1609, the ring of Saturn was described as two handles (*ansae*). It was not until 1656 that the ring was interpreted correctly by the Dutch scientist Christiaan Huygens, who illustrated his findings in his *Systema saturnium*, published in 1659 (fig. 40c). In the same work, Huygens illustrated several earlier observations of Saturn (fig. 40d), all of which indicate the advanced state of the depiction in Van Wynen's painting.[9] The four small spheres that surround Saturn may represent its moons, which were first discovered during the seventeenth century.[10]

In Van Wynen's painting, one cannot be certain of the identification of all the planets shown between Saturn and the earth since only four are represented when in fact there should be five. The largest of these spheres appears to be Venus, the brightest star. It is shown reflecting light onto the earth. The two planets to the right of it appear to be Mars and Jupiter, the latter of which always stands next to Saturn. Only one heavenly body, probably Mercury or possibly the moon, can be seen between Earth and Venus.

Considering its complex iconography, one can assume that Van Wynen's painting was intended for a cultivated audience. It is not known whether the painting was done as a commission; nor is it known whether its often obscure symbolism is based directly on some philosophical writing of the period. Nevertheless, it is interesting to see how the artist has combined two major concerns of the late seventeenth century: scientific investigation and theological interpretation.

40c Saturn's ring, as drawn by Christiaan Huygens, from his *Systema saturnium*, . . . , (The Hague: Adrian Vlacq, 1659), p. 24 (Photo: Yale University Library)

1 Of these paintings, the best known and the one that shows the closest similarity in treatment of figures is *The Temptation of St. Anthony* (oil on canvas, 74 x 74 cm), National Gallery of Ireland, Dublin, no. 527. The Dublin picture and another signed work, an allegory (oil on canvas, 37 x 47 cm), last recorded with a Munich art dealer, are both illustrated in W. Bernt, *Die niederlandischen Maler des 17. Jahrhunderts*, 4 vols. (Munich: F. Bruckmann, 1948–62), 4: nos. 332,333. A pair of allegorical paintings (oil on canvas, 44.5 x 52 cm) incorporating cosmic imagery was sold by Christie's, 31 July 1931, no. 31 (Photo: Witt).

2 An alternative solution to the meaning of these spheres is that they represent planets. See in particular the representations on star charts of the period, as, for example, Karel Allard's star chart of the southern hemisphere calculated for the year 1700, illustrated in R. A. Skelton, *Decorative Printed Maps of the 15th to 18th Centuries* (London: Spring Books, 1965), pl. 72.

3 For the interpretation of the Hebraic letters, I am grateful to Prof. George H. Williams of the Divinity School, Harvard University.

4 The angels immediately to the left of Christ carry the cross, chalice, scourge, and crown of thorns. An angel farther to the left holds a cloth that may represent the cloth of the tomb or the veil of Veronica. Another angel, at the upper left, bears a club, which may also be connected with Christ's passion, symbolizing Judas's betrayal of Christ as foreshadowed by Cain's killing of Abel.

5 The royal robe, crown and sceptor symbolize Christ's role as king. The palm branch refers to his victory over death. The snake in the form of a circle with its tail in its mouth symbolizes eternity. The meaning of the flaming sword is unclear. It is traditionally the attribute of Jophiel, the guardian of the tree of knowledge; see Genesis 3:24.

6 See John 1:4–9, 3:19–21, 8:12, 9:5, 12:35–36, and 12:46.

7 The incomplete inscription on the book should probably be read EVANGEL(ICUM SECUN)/ DUM (JOANNEM) ("the gospel according to John").

8 I am grateful to Dr. E. Dekker of the Rijksmuseum voor de Geschiedenis van de Natuurwetenschappen en van de Geneeskunde, Leiden, for assisting me in interpreting the artist's depiction of the solar system.

9 The representation of the stars should also be considered post-Galileo since they are not shown at a fixed distance from the earth as they are in astronomical charts produced before the invention of the telescope.

10 The moons of Saturn that had been discovered by the end of the 17th century were Titan (discovered in 1655), Iapetus (1671), Rhea (1672), Dione (1684), and Tethys (1684). The two moons to the left of Saturn may represent two of the four moons of Jupiter that were known during the 17th century: Io, Europa, Ganymede, and Callisto, all discovered by Galileo and Marius in 1610.

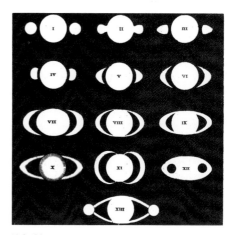

40d Observations of Saturn's ring made between 1610 and 1650 by Galileo, G. Riccioli, J. Hevel, P. Gassendi, and others, from Christiaan Huygens's *Systema saturnium*, . . . (The Hague: Adrian Vlacq, 1659) (Photo: Yale University Library)

Index of Artists

Designed by Logowitz + Moore Associates, Boston
Typography by Dix Typesetting Co. Inc., Syracuse
Printed by Thomas Todd Company, Boston